Books Published by Ready, Set, Go! Publishing

The Start-Up Guide for Opening, Remodeling & Running
a Successful Beauty Salon

A Salon Owner's Guide to Wealth

The Salon Building Bible

The Modern Salon in Pictures

How to Offer 5-Star Service at Your Salon
and Make Big Money!

The Start-Up Guide for Opening, Remodeling & Running
a Successful Barbershop

Barbershop Now!

Cosmetology School Graduate - 1 Business Lessons

Cosmetology School Graduate - 2 Life Lessons

Cosmetology School Graduate - 3 How to get a J.O.B. in a Salon

READY, SET, GO! BOOKS

HOW TO OFFER
5-STAR SERVICE
AT YOUR SALON

AND MAKE BIG MONEY!

Jeff Grissler and Eric Ryant

Ready, Set, Go!

**How to Offer 5-Star Service at Your Salon
and Make Big Money!**

First edition.

ISBN: 978-0-9911584-0-9 (paperback)
ISBN: 978-0-9911584-1-6 (digital)

Published in the U.S. by Ready Set Go Publishing, LLC
215 Pascal Street
Fort Collins, Colorado 80524

Printed in the United States of America

Go to www. readysetgopublishing.com to purchase other Ready, Set, Go! books.

Table of Contents

PART I: What Does it Mean to be a 5-Star Service Provider?

1. Love to Go There, But…   1
2. What Customers Expect from a 5-Star Salon   3
3. Learning from 5-Star Leaders in Other Industries   7
4. How to Get Your Staff to Understand VIP Service   11

PART II: First Impressions: the Look of the Salon

5. What You See is What You Get   17
6. Don't Get Bored with the Basics   23
7. Why It's Important to Remodel Your Salon   27
8. Front Desk Greatness   31

PART III: Good Customer Communications in the Salon

9. It Starts with the Greeting   35
10. It Continues Throughout the Visit   41
11. Salon Talk   45
12. Dealing With and Resolving Conflict   51
13. How to Say "No"   57

PART IV: Communication with Customers Outside the Salon

14. Branding your Salon   63
15. Contacting Your Customers   65
16. Marketing Your Salon Online   69

PART V: Customer Retention

17. VIP Service Only Starts with Their Name   73
18. Keeping Clients for Life   75

19. The VVIP Customers   79
20. VIP Service for Males in the Salon   83

PART VI: Quality Products Complement Quality Service

21. Selecting the Right Products for Your Salon   87
22. The Importance of Vendor Relationships   91

PART VII: A 5-Star Staff

23. How to Hire Quality Service Providers   97
24. The Importance of the Gatekeeper   101

PART VIII: Keeping it Going

25. Maintaining the Right Attitude   109
26. 5-Star for Life   111

Introduction

Every successful salon owner understands that top-notch service is critical to business profitability and longevity. In this new edition of the Ready, Set, Go! Beauty Book series, we show you how to differentiate your business by providing 5-star service. We help you understand the fundamentals and true meaning of customer service—what customers want, deserve and expect—and how to win customer loyalty by delivering the ultimate customer experience.

This book is designed to educate you as the salon owner, manager, or employee on what 5-star service in your salon should be. It's also intended to be a tool that every one of your employees can use to improve their customer service. This book will get you thinking about the little things that make a difference in customer service and have you itching to continue the "wow" experience one customer at a time, every time.

So what is 5-star service? What do your clients expect when they walk through your salon's entrance? Do you and your staff truly understand what they are expecting? Can you deliver?

If everyone in your salon, you included, understands the meaning of 5-star, luxury service then you can deliver an experience like no one around. Service is service, but giving it the right way is another story. Let's take a look at the definitions of 5-star service by industry experts from around the world.

"Something that is an indulgence rather than a necessity, sumptuous or expensive, abundance and done with great ease and comfort."

CEO, Ritz Carlton

"A 5-star experience is something that simply makes me feel good—hotel, restaurant, salon or spa—it doesn't matter. This experience, in order to be five-star must have the physical presence and amenities and extend to the all-important levels of service."

John Harms
CEO, Harms Software

"Five-star service is an experience. It's the total package. One of my friends once told me, 'It's what I deserve'. I think that's pretty close to a perfect definition."

Cal Simmons
Chairman, www.FiveStarAlliance.com

"When needs and desires are anticipated and fulfilled even before being realized to the extent that they become a requirement."

Christie Gaderson
Priorities Concierge

"Quality service, by definition, means something that appears to be the best of whatever it represents. It's a word that raises people's expectations, whether talking about clothing for women or locations for people to live . . . You pay for recognition, but probably the most important thing it represents is delivery on the promise of the brand's name."

Isadore Sharp
Founder, Chairman & CEO, Four Seasons Hotels & Resorts

"Five-star is defined by attention to the details. Meticulous workmanship, sumptuous atmosphere and discerning good taste."

Robert Mackasek
CEO, Valera Global

"Luxury means total serenity."

Herve Van der Straeten
Furniture Designer

"Luxury is style and comfort, priced accordingly. Extravagance is style and comfort, cost be damned."

Tod Herbers
Publisher, Home and Design Magazine

"5-star service—to me luxury is simply the best of the best. The finest quality and exceeded expectations in any area. The service is exquisite with supreme taste. In regard to the service that we provide, luxury is living without limits and having your time and peace to it ALL at the highest level."

Reginald Roberson
CEO, Lavish Lifestyles, LLC

"Luxury is . . . uniqueness, exclusivity, these are luxury to me. Also, to be happy is a luxury. You could put me in the most beautiful place, but if I'm not happy, I'll want to leave."

Bruno Frisoni
Accessories Designer

"Five-star services . . . can be defined by consistent superior quality with an element of uniqueness and exclusivity. A stay experience that I can boldly share and recommend to people within my inner circle. A stay experience that will make me feel 'very special' from arrival to departure and beyond. As a General Manager, selection of associates who are genuinely delighted to please others is an essential quality that I seek. The consistency of our brand elements must be maintained at all times to provide continuity of the 'best Westin experience' for our guests from one Hotel to another. In my experience, this consistency of brand values and unparalleled personal service will drive customer loyalty that is 'beyond reason.' This to me is luxury service."

John Varghese
General Manager, The Westin Alexandria

"To me luxury is defined as the best that life has to offer: an endless supply of amenities, a legendary setting, wondrous tranquility, spectacular scenery and the opportunity to embrace each moment because every need has been satisfied."

Jose Luis Mogollon
Director of Development, Quivira Los Cabos

"The word service is overused and often ambiguous. True five-star delivers unexpected pleasures above and beyond what is essential or necessary. It exists in the small details that differentiate an experience from what is 'normal' or 'average'."

Michael McFadden
Co-Founder, The Society of Leisure Enthusiasts

"I define quality service as the details that exceed your expectations and please the five senses. It's the touch and feel of fine linens or a plush robe. It's in the taste of fresh herbs and ingredients. It's the quality sound of live music. It's the beauty and fragrance of fresh flowers."

Sheila Beal
Editor, www.GoVisitHawaii.com

If there is one thing you can learn from the quotes above, it is that 5-star service is more than your salon's front entrance or the person that sits behind your reception desk. It's not just your salon's website, or a phone number or an option on a pre-recorded phone menu. Yes, all these things are important and do have a cumulative impact, but what is essential is that service is not seen as a chore—it's the responsibility of everyone in your salon or spa organization, from the CEO to the person sweeping the floor. Your salon team must be focused on one common goal: no matter what the position or job title, serve customers with such consistency, integrity, creativity, and sincerity that they will have no choice but to keep coming back for more, and eagerly recommend your business to friends, families and colleagues.

In today's highly competitive salon and spa marketplace, a business needs more than excellent products, good technical service, efficient procedures, and competitive prices to give the ultimate 5-star experience. It also needs to connect with its customers through authentic, human-to-human interactions that satisfy not only their practical needs, but their emotional wants as well. We never said that owning your own salon/spa business would be easy, but let us take you on a 5-star journey that will set your salon business apart from all the salons in your area.

PART I

What Does it Mean to Be a 5-Star Service Provider?

CHAPTER 1

Love to Go There, But . . .

"Your most unhappy customers are your greatest source of learning."

– Bill Gates

The color, style and cut you and your team offer may be second to none, but that doesn't make you a 5-star salon. As salon owners, we must continually strive to make the services we offer better than anyone else in town. We should constantly think of ways to create the ultimate service experience. There are many things to consider when trying to give the ultimate 5-star experience every time your customer walks through the salon door. Have you ever thought about how hard it is to do business with your company? Confused, not understanding where I am going with this? Let me give you a scenario to think about.

Example - Have you gone out to dinner and had the most wonderful meal ever, but you went through hell to get it? You tried to call and make reservations for months but you kept getting put on hold for what seemed like eternity. Once you finally made reservations, it was weeks away from when you wanted to go. Finally the night came and you pulled up to the restaurant to find the parking garage was full and you had to walk a mile in heels to get to the restaurant in the rain. Once you got there, your reservation had been lost and you had to wait at the bar three-deep for almost an hour. Finally you were seated, your waiter said he would be right back and disappeared for what seemed like another hour. You finally got your food and it was so over-the-top it was amazing! Every bite was fabulous. After all was said and done, you paid your bill (expensive) and left. Was it 5-star service, and will you be back again? My guess is maybe, maybe not. But it sure didn't live up to the complete 5-star rave everyone said it had.

Similarly, your product may be amazing; your end result - color, style, cut - may be great, but if the whole customer experience is not exceptional, you're not a 5-star salon. This book does not teach you how to give a top-notch cut, there are a lot of classes for that. This book focuses on how to give a top-notch salon experience.

CHAPTER 2

What Customers Expect from a 5-Star Salon

"The first step in exceeding customer's expectations it to know those expectations."

– Roy H. Williams

Does your salon give a lasting impression? Does your client leave and tell her friends and family she had the most unbelievable experience at the salon or does she say she got her hair cut and colored today? Nothing special, nothing noted, nothing to share with everyone she makes contact with that day. Lesson learned here. My guess is your salon is not offering any treatments or services that are different than your competitors', and certainly not 5-star service.

While you can't control what your competitors do, you can minimize their impact on your business by what you do. It's all about standing apart from the rest. What makes your salon business different from the one next door, across the street or around the corner is all based on one thing: service. How you service the customer will make your business stand out from any competitor.

Have you actually thought about the service levels in your salon? Are you happy with the way you and your staff handle customers? Do customers perceive your service levels as being different from your competitors? Better, worse, or adequate for the price point you are charging? Do you feel that your staff always does more than required when working and performing a service for a guest? If you have to think about any of these questions, then the answer is no!

Define What Your Salon May Be Missing

I have moved between various cities around the country and through my job, and visited many salons through my travels as a customer, consultant and friend. I have had different services in many of these salons. Most of the stylists who cut my hair have been extremely talented, but I have to say that over the years I have only been "wowed" and treated with 5-star service once or twice. In fact, I have never been formally asked if I wanted to buy a hair product or if I was happy with the haircut. Is my hair that perfect? Not! In most cases it is assumed that I am happy and I leave without so much as a handshake or a thank you. Does this happen in your salon?

In order to understand what your salon is missing, you first have to identify what your customers expect when it comes to high caliber customer service. In a recent customer service workshop I conducted for high-end salons and spas, we discussed the importance of 5-star service in a tough economy. But what does 5-star service really mean? In order to give that level of service, it is important to understand what customers think it means and what they expect from you in the salon or spa.

Take a look at what customers actually say 5-star service should be at a salon or spa:

- Impeccable customer service
- Helpful staff throughout the entire visit
- An unparalleled experience that you feel good about, even entertained with, and you find value in the service or product offered
- Top-notch service is when you feel the staff delivers without asking for it—almost like they are reading our minds because they know us so well
- Staff resolves any issue immediately
- Staff makes the customer feel special
- Big greeting when they enter the salon or spa like they are family
- Genuine friendliness, smiles, and personality
- Must feel like you are getting your money's worth
- Rewarding with some type of customer loyalty
- Staff dressed for success, giving the feeling that they are in a fashion forward environment
- The newest retail products available in the marketplace

- Ambiance throughout the space
- Secrets to be shared with the service provider but not with anyone else
- Intuitive to the needs of the client and understanding how to deliver the service
- If retail is purchased, explain in detail how to use at home over and over again until the customer leaves with a true understanding of the product
- Knowing what services and color were used on the last visit
- Guest feels like a human being, not a number
- Fixes a problem without fuss even though it was my fault

This survey shows that customers are looking for a good experience and to get what they ask for with no surprises. They are not asking us as salon or spa owners to build a new luxurious space for millions of dollars; in fact, what they ask should cost nothing as business owners. It's putting the proper procedures in place to ensure 5-star service on all levels throughout your salon or spa.

The most important thing to remember is that you have to understand the guest so that you can better serve them. You have to recognize their needs, be attentive to what they say and not how they act toward you, so you can provide an appropriate response. The key is to always try to give a meaningful experience and not just a product. It's about making each client special.

CHAPTER 3

Learning from 5-Star Leaders in Other Industries

"Price is what you pay. Value is what you get."
— Warren Buffett

If you are wondering how service levels make an impact on customers, let's look at how airlines and hotels gear their service levels, five stars being the best. There are not many airlines or hotels in the world that are rated five stars, but those that are work extremely hard to maintain that 5-star status. Their company profits are based on customers frequenting their businesses because they receive 5-star services each and every time they visit. These guests expect nothing but 5-star service and they are willing to pay for it.

Classes in the Sky

What's happening above the clouds mirrors what's happening on the ground. For many of us flying has become a more like a trip in a cattle car. Many people are sandwiched into their seats with their knees hitting the back of the seat in front of them—uncomfortable is an understatement. The flight attendant hastily rushes down the aisles giving us a splash of water, coffee, or soda in a plastic cup with a tiny bag of peanuts, chips, or a Luna bar. The cabin is strewn with candy wrappers, newspapers, magazines, and cracked plastic glasses. Welcome to economy, or should I say every day, service. You expect the same every time you fly. Do your customers feel that way when they enter your salon? Does your salon offer the same service every time, nothing unusual, nothing special?

Now let's take a look on "the other side of the curtain": first class, where

5-star service is offered. The seats are so comfortable that one may lie almost horizontal if they feel they need a nap while traveling. The flight attendant is offering cocktails in fine stemware with a linen napkin. I forgot to mention the hot towel that was offered to clean off the travel grime one gets when touching everything in the airport. Oh so nice! Now the dinner is served. A choice of dinner, I may add. Hot food served on bone china with real silverware, not plastic forks and knives. More wine, of course! The flight attendant stops by every few minutes to ask if all is well and offer more wine, water, anything to make the trip more pleasant. There is such a big difference in client service when one expects it, or should I say, is used to it.

Ground Service Above Board

Why should service be any different on the ground? Service in the sky or on the ground must be consistent. Luxury 5-star hotels offer the highest level of service and comfort, sure to please even the most discriminating tastes. Guests enjoy top-notch amenities, elegant accommodations and the staff is so trained at customer service that is almost impossible to have a bad stay. Most guests remember the staff because it is the staff that makes the experience, not the glitz of the hotel. Sure that helps, but did you ever hear anyone say that they came back to the hotel for the beauty of the hotel? Okay, so you may have heard that, but most of the time it's because of the level of how well you were treated as a guest, the food you had at the hotel restaurant, the way you were checked in, the bellhop using your first and last name when he escorted you to your room, and the valet, when he took your car keys, the bed turned down with chocolates on your pillow. The experience wins every time.

In order to truly understand what 5-star service is about, I invite you to read the philosophy of one of the most highly respected hotel chains in the world – the Ritz Carlton. Their mission, to give the customer exactly what they came for, is why they have the highest return customer rate in the world.

The Ritz Carlton Creed

The Ritz-Carlton Hotel is a place where the genuine care and comfort of our guests is our highest mission.

We pledge to provide the finest personal service and facilities for our guests who will always enjoy a warm, relaxed, yet refined ambience.

The Ritz-Carlton experience enlivens the senses, instills well-being, and fulfills even the unexpressed wishes and needs of our guests.

Motto

At The Ritz-Carlton Hotel Company, L.L.C., "We are Ladies and Gentlemen serving Ladies and Gentlemen." This motto exemplifies the anticipatory service provided by all staff members.

Three Steps of Service

- A warm and sincere greeting. Use the guest's name.
- Anticipation and fulfillment of each guest's needs.
- Fond farewell. Give a warm good-bye and use the guest's name.

Service Values: I Am Proud To Be Ritz-Carlton

1. I build strong relationships and create Ritz-Carlton guests for life.
2. I am always responsive to the expressed and unexpressed wishes and needs of our guests.
3. I am empowered to create unique, memorable and personal experiences for our guests.
4. I understand my role in achieving the Key Success Factors, embracing Community Footprints and creating The Ritz-Carlton Mystique.
5. I continuously seek opportunities to innovate and improve The Ritz-Carlton experience.
6. I own and immediately resolve guest problems.
7. I create a work environment of teamwork and lateral service so that the needs of our guests and each other are met.
8. I have the opportunity to continuously learn and grow.
9. I am involved in the planning of the work that affects me.
10. I am proud of my professional appearance, language and behavior.
11. I protect the privacy and security of our guests, my fellow employees and the company's confidential information and assets.
12. I am responsible for uncompromising levels of cleanliness and creating a safe and accident-free environment.

The Employee Promise

At The Ritz-Carlton, our Ladies and Gentlemen are the most important resource in our service commitment to our guests.

By applying the principles of trust, honesty, respect, integrity and commitment, we nurture and maximize talent to the benefit of each individual and the company.

The Ritz-Carlton fosters a work environment where diversity is valued, quality of life is enhanced, individual aspirations are fulfilled, and The Ritz-Carlton Mystique is strengthened.

No matter what type of business you are in - airline, hotel, or salon/spa - quality service is quality service and the level of service you offer is up to you.

CHAPTER 4

How to Get Your Staff to Understand VIP Service

"I believe that our background and our circumstances may have influenced who we are, but we are responsible for who we become."

– Rita Ghatourey

In today's world, different people perceive VIP service differently. You have to take into consideration many factors which segregate how people think and how they look at things in general; for example, our social upbringing, where we went to school, what we eat, where we go on vacation, what side of town we grew up on and what social class we were born into. It all comes down to what each of us is used to, what we like, and how we are treated throughout the course of our lives.

Each of these factors dramatically influences how we perceive things in life and how we react to special situations at work, at home, and in social environments. We all look at things from the perspective of what we like, what we desire, and how we expect to be treated. The way we treat others is based on how we have been treated in life. Since we do not all come from the same set of circumstances, you, the salon owner, cannot expect your employees to understand how you perceive VIP service unless you get everyone on the same page of what VIP should be in your eyes.

In life we only know what we are taught, what we see, what the people around us do. In order for your salon team to understand VIP, you have to be their teacher. You need to mentor them on your perception of ultimate VIP service.

Elisha Wendt of Blush Salon tells the story of the frustration she felt early in her career trying to get her team to offer VIP service to each of her salon's clients. She would continually watch mistakes and mishandling of clients. She would sit the employee down and try to explain what she thought was wrong and how to correct the situation, but the reaction she got was like a deer in headlights. Needless to say, they didn't seem to get it and neither did she. She didn't know how to get through to her team.

One day in a salon team meeting, one of her stylists said that she had gone out to a 5-star restaurant for her birthday, and the food was amazing. She went on and on about the service and food. Wendt looked at her and said, "I must go to this restaurant! Where is it?" To her disbelief, the stylist named a national chain restaurant. This chain is in every town across the country, and is certainly not a 5-star establishment. It's probably more in the category of a quick stop for a burger and beer on the way home from work. Yet, this was the stylist's perception of 5-star, VIP service.

A light popped on in Wendt's head. She was surprised she hadn't figured this out before. She then asked each of her team members what they thought was the best restaurant in town with the best service. She could not believe the answers. Who loved the local pizza place, Chick-fil-A, Ruby Tuesday? If the staff thought this was 5-star food and great service, how would they know truly 5-star services in the salon? In their eyes this was the best. Wendt realized it was up to her to show them what she perceived to be VIP best service and the difference. Similarly, you may have to show, rather than tell, your staff how to be 5-star.

VIP Salon Team Service Questions

Ask yourself and the salon staff the following questions:
- What is your favorite restaurant?
- How were you treated in the restaurant, and did you like it?
- What is your favorite fast food restaurant, and why?
- What is your favorite place to go shopping?
- What is your favorite clothing store?
- What is your favorite hotel to stay in, and why?
- Which magazines do you subscribe to?
- Do you prefer internet shopping or onsite shopping?

- Have you ever been to a country club?
- Have you ever been to a resort?
- Have you flown first class?
- Have you shopped and/or visited a high-end jewelry store?
- Have you ridden in a limo?
- Have you visited a Mercedes or other high-end car dealership?

Once you're finished with the questions, sit with your staff and evaluate what everyone had to say. Evaluate the responses and compare them to your own. You can take this one step further and ask some of your guests to fill out a questionnaire with the same questions. I am sure you will be surprised at the answers you receive. In my personal experience, some of my staff had in fact never been treated with a VIP service in their lives. They had never been to a high-end restaurant, flown first class, been in a Mercedes car, stayed in a luxurious resort, or simply shopped in a high-end department store and, if you can believe this, never had their nails done or received a massage! So how in the world could you expect them to offer VIP service to someone any more than you would expect them to read or speak French without being fluent in the language?

Salon Team Gets Some VIP!

Now it's up to you to educate your staff and get them on board with VIP service. Okay, how do you do this and get it done as quickly as possible, so you can set the stage for a quick lesson in VIP?

The first thing you must realize is that this is an investment, and it will cost you some out-of-pocket money. It will be a long-term investment with results over time, so don't think you will see immediate financial results. I call this business development.

I have put together a list of things you can do with your staff that that will make an immediate impact and give them a better understanding of VIP service.

- Take your team to the best restaurant in town. If you have a local steak house they normally give the highest quality product and service. Call the owner in advance and explain what you are trying to accomplish. I am sure he will be happy to accommodate you. Have everyone watch, listen, and learn from the moment they walk in the door and are greeted by the host, the busboy, the waiter. Have them observe the people sitting around them. Watch how the drinks, appetizers, and main entrees are delivered to the table. Did the manager or owner visit the table? What did they say? Did they thank you for the visit? I am sure they did. The entire experience should demonstrate VIP service. When you leave, your staff will have a better understanding of service, fine food, and yes, VIP treatment.

- Take your team to the finest hotel in town. If you don't have one, then find one in a neighboring city. This should be at least a 4-star hotel. From the moment they drive up to valet the car to the time they arrive in the room, the experience should impress your staff. The valet, baggage person, and front desk personnel should give them a show that exemplifies VIP service and helps them understand what they should be offering to their own clients. Once in the room they should see how the bellman brings up your bags. Did he use your last name? Did she ask to hang your clothes, get you ice, explain the restaurant in the hotel and where the gym is located? Did he or she ask if you needed anything else before leaving? I am sure they did. Have your staff open the closet. Are there slippers, a robe, and maybe an umbrella in the closet for your use? I am sure there are, if you look. How does your team feel? I am willing to bet they feel like they are VIPs . . . how could they not? You now should be starting to understand what we are preaching: VIP has to be taught, and you can't expect your staff to get it without someone showing them. (By the way, here's another idea if treating your whole team to an overnight hotel experience is just too cost prohibitive. Get one room, take the whole team to experience the service the staff provides and see the room, then give the room to one employee for the night. This could be done as a drawing or a reward for something such as selling the most retail in a month; better yet, have your staff give the room away to the person they think does the best job with their clients.)

- Visit a high-end spa in your area and have your team get spa treatments. Let them notice how you are welcomed into the spa. Were you greeted in a professional manner? Were you asked if you wanted water, coffee, or something to eat? Were you seated in a waiting area? Were you taken to the dressing room and given a robe and slippers? I am sure all of this was done in more than a professional manner. Once again, make sure your staff notices everything about the décor, service, cleanliness, and most importantly, how the service provider handles them. The last thing, and one of the most important, is the retail push and the checkout. Make sure they pay very close attention to the detail and the handling of the final checkout. This should be the ultimate VIP service.

Evaluate and VIP Like Crazy!

In my experience, if you invested the time and money into any of the lessons above, your team will now have a true understanding of VIP service. You allowed them to experience something they never have. Maybe you haven't experienced these things yourself, so you have now set the stage for everyone who works for you to emulate what they experienced. How can they fail? They are now all on board. You must evaluate your service every day, week and month. The investment you make in your staff by doing these special events, or "business developments," will only benefit you over time. The more energy, and yes, money you put into your team, the more you will improve the overall VIP service in your salon. The lesson learned here is that VIP starts with how you perceive it yourself. If you have never been taught French you can't expect to speak the language. It is no different with VIP service. Teach your staff to speak the VIP language!

What Does it Mean to Be a 5-Star Service Provider?

★ 5-star is about more than a great end product, it's about a great overall experience.

★ In order to be perceived at 5-star, you have to understand what customers think that means and what they expect from a 5-star salon.

★ Airlines and hotels that have earned the 5-star rating set a good example of how to treat customers.

★ Your staff may have to experience 5-star service themselves before they can give it to others.

★ Ultimately the level of service you offer is up to you; decide today to become 5-star and get ready to set yourself apart from the competition.

PART II

First Impressions: The Look of the Salon

CHAPTER 5

What You See is What You Get

"You never get a second chance to make a good first impression."

– Will Rogers

We've all heard about the importance of a good first impression. Customers (or potential customers) who come to your salon will be impacted by what they see. Clients visit your salon to be made beautiful, and they have confidence that will happen if they see beauty when they walk in. If you find it hard to believe that a beautiful salon can instill confidence, maybe it's easier to believe that if they see an outdated or sloppy salon, they will certainly start having doubts about their upcoming service! What the customer sees when they enter is the first test of a 5-star salon, from having the right décor, to keeping the front desk and retail sections clutter free, to the importance of a spotless salon and professional looking staff.

The coolest furnishings in the world won't help if you're not also focused on the little things, so let's start there. Many business owners claim that they offer 5-star services in their salon business, but do they truly do the little things that make a difference to the client? As owners and managers, they talk the talk to their staff about the little things that make the salon different and how they should act and approach customers as service providers. But do they actually walk the walk and really notice and understand the subtleties of what customers see? The survival of your salon's business may be riding on it.

Owners and salon managers need to understand that it's the small-scale neglect and little service problems that often lead to bigger issues.

Example - A guest walks into the salon and has to sit on a magazine-strewn couch because the area has not been cleaned since the last guest. The guest sets her handbag down next to her and she places it on spilled coffee. The guest asks where the restroom is and no one responds, so she awkwardly finds her own way to the restroom to clean her handbag. When she gets there she finds no tissues or toilet paper in the bathroom. The lock to the restroom is broken and she has to hold the handle to keep the door closed. Once she closes the door she notices the light bulb is out and has to use her cell phone light to get around.

None of these individual issues may seem like large problems, but it's the little things that snowball into bigger problems. In this example the customer is expecting 5-star service—this is the talk you supposedly talk and what your customers are expecting—but in this case you and your salon team missed the little things in a BIG way.

Little Problems Become Big Problems

Large organizations like the Ritz Carlton, Disneyland, Mercedes and Lexus dealers, and thousands of other businesses pick up trash, polish counters, greet customers with big hello's, straighten displays, and keep their bathrooms spotless. These companies know it's the little things that make their customers' experience with them a memorable one for all the right reasons, not just the services they provide. They have great insight on customer satisfaction. Their 5-star approaches have enabled them to be leaders in the business world globally.

When details are overlooked and little things are no longer noticed and left to fester, they can breed indifference and sloppiness on a much grander scale among your staff. Let's look at the example we used above. It's highly unlikely that all of the circumstances in the example above could happen at once, but what if they did, not just with one guest but with a few? If you, as the owner or manager didn't seem to care, then you couldn't expect your staff to either.

- Why did no one notice the reception area was dirty and coffee was spilled on the floor?
- Why did no one mop the coffee and tidy the magazine area?
- Why did no one at the front desk direct the customer to the restroom, or better yet assist with cleaning the coffee off her bag?
- Why did no one say pardon the mess, and let me assist you?
- Why did no one replace the tissues or toilet paper in the restroom?
- Why did no one notice and change the light bulb in the restroom?
- Why did no one fix the broken lock on the restroom door?

These little things immediately become larger once you start realizing you are losing customers. Have you, as the owner or manager, noticed any of the above issues in your salon? Think about it. If you noticed them even once and didn't address and correct them immediately, why would your staff do so? In this case, your team is looking for guidance and guidance comes from the leader. One of the Ritz Carlton Service Values listed in an earlier chapter was, "I own and immediately resolve guest problems." Own it and teach your staff to own it too.

Paying attention as an owner or manager is a lot more than being a janitor. Yes, it is important that your staff sees you as Mr. or Ms. Clean, but they must also see what your customers see. It is your job to help them develop the same set of eyes you have for the little things that count. It's the little details that incorporate the 5-star experience. One set of eyes is great, but to be successful it has to be more than the eyes of the owner or manager. Can you imagine the effect if your whole team had eyes for the 5-star setting? In order to have everyone on board, walk every employee through the salon to see what the customer sees, touches, and feels while visiting the salon. Then train them how to keep the salon in tip-top shape, always setting an example yourself.

Understanding the little things and incorporating this process into your salon's vision is a big accomplishment. Once you get everyone on board and get your staff to not only talk the talk but to walk the walk, you have truly accomplished what it takes to make little things part of the 5-star experience. When you incorporate this level of care and attention to every detail, your salon guests will notice and appreciate it. They will feel a sense of pride in being associated with your organization, and will be proud to refer their friends to your business.

Little Additions Make a Big Impression

Once you have any little problems under control - that is, they're fixed almost instantly so they're never really a problem - you know they can't negatively impact your customers' first impressions. Now it's time to take that extra step to positively impact their first impression. We're still not talking about major renovations, rather those little things that can set you apart. Here are some examples that can take a clean, friendly, nice establishment to a 5-star stunner:

- Fresh flowers at your front reception desk
- Glass bowl of Godiva candies at your front desk
- Glass bowl of fruit at your front desk
- Hand sanitizer and hand lotion at your front desk
- Water, tea, wine, coffee served at all times
- Hand sanitizer mounted on various spots throughout the salon
- Current magazines throughout the salon
- Robes available for guests
- Umbrellas available at front entrance
- Valet parking if necessary
- IPads for customer use
- Linen towels with salon logo in bathrooms in place of paper towels with hamper
- Hand sanitizer/hand lotion in bathroom
- Wall mounted makeup mirror with light in bathrooms
- Candles in bathroom
- Samples of hair sprays or products in bathrooms
- Retail samples at reception desk as giveaways
- Travel coffee cups to go with salons name
- All bags for retail branded with salons name

Start thinking of how you can make that "wow" first impression, get off on the right foot with your customers, and set your salon apart from the competition.

CHAPTER 6

Don't Get Bored With the Basics

"People are more likely to believe you and like you when you know you look fine."

— Estee Lauder

When it comes to the daily things we do in life, we sometimes lose track of what is important. Let's face it, sometimes it is easier to avoid doing the things we know are good for us if they take a few extra minutes in a day—like going to the gym or eating at home instead of on the go. It's so easy to promise you'll start tomorrow or next week or you'll eventually get back on track, eat right, and go to the gym.

Like going to the gym or eating right, offering 5-star service in your salon is no different. It's easy to get bored with the basics and forget about the things that are important to you and your customers.

Great companies and successful individuals keep a keen eye on the basics all the time. Like great athletes, they know that mastering the fundamentals makes all the difference between success and failure. You can't expect to hit a game-winning home run without mastering everything else that goes along with swinging the bat. In business, the seemingly small things are easy to overlook, but they can set your company apart from the competition and in turn improve your sales, your repeat business, and your bottom line. Why is this so important? Because it's the basics that your neighboring salon or spa overlooks—the small things that turn out to be big things. Mastering them will continue to set your salon or spa business apart from the rest.

Cleanliness is Next to Godliness

I visited a spa while on vacation. The first thing I noticed was how the staff was dressed. They all dressed professionally and looked beautiful. Each carried themselves in a professional manner.

When I entered the reception area I was impressed by the way the receptionist welcomed me. She asked my name, where I was staying and if I was having a good day. She never lost eye contact with me and had a perpetual smile that would not go away. I'm sure this was her standard approach with each guest, but the way she did it and said it—with sincerity—made me feel as if I was the first person she had ever asked these questions.

She then walked me to a beautiful, spotless waiting area. The magazine rack looked like it had been reorganized alphabetically after the last guest. She offered me a choice of several beverages, and walked over to an area with a sanitizer on the wall. She carefully used disinfectant hand wash before she touched the glass to make me a drink. This lovely girl wiped my glass with a clean napkin before she poured my drink, then handed me a hand wipe, cloth napkin and my special concoction of cucumber and water. Wow! I was completely overwhelmed with the experience and I hadn't even set foot in the spa area! This employee obviously hadn't gotten bored with the "basics" of 5-star customer service.

Let's take a look at my experience. What can be more basic than a salon or spa's employees dressed for success? The staff looked clean and sharp - makeup on and ready for business.

What is more basic than a receptionist's welcoming smile? Her questions about my day, her interest, style and graciousness may have been rehearsed, but I loved it.

What is more basic than the receptionist washing her hands with hand sanitizer? She was actually worried about passing germs on to the spa's new guest. Amazing! And who had thought about putting a hand sanitizer next to the guest waiting area? These little things - let's call them basics - added to the total impact of the guest experience. It was genius!

If you look good you play good, and if you play good everyone wins!

The close cousins of cleanliness are personal appearance and hygiene.

Again, this is about as basic as it gets. Losing control of your salon or spa's dress code can happen very quickly.

There is a reason that Chanel employees wear white lab coats at high-end department stores. It's because they give the shopper the appearance of professionalism, almost the impression of being a doctor. If they're in white lab coats they must know what they're doing, right? They command respect, making almost anything they say believable. Most Chanel employees even have the same (almost clone-like) look, too: hair tied back in a bun, makeup done to the nines, and a sleek, model-like appearance and figure. Chanel has not forgotten about the basics of dress code, appearance and hygiene, and neither should you at your salon. The Chanel "look" personifies 5-star products and service. Their employee dress code is one of the small things that makes their brand a force in the fragrance industry. Remember, this is about not forgetting the basics. Dress code is one of the most important basics your salon and spa must insist upon.

Every salon business is different. Each company has its own standards for appearance which fit its location, its image and the customs of its clientele. A high-end salon and spa in the New York's East Village may have a trendier look than a salon or spa on located in the Plaza Hotel on Fifth Avenue in New York City. Both places require specific dress codes, but they will be quite different.

My mother once told me that it is always better to be overdressed than underdressed. I believe this philosophy is also true in the salon and spa business, whatever the address; being a tad bit overdressed gives the perception of an upscale place of business. My advice is to always go for the overdressed, professional look. It symbolizes competence, intelligence, preparation, and character, and these are major factors in how the customer, consciously or not, evaluates your business.

CHAPTER 7

Why It's Important to Remodel Your Salon

"Fashions fade, style is eternal."

– Yves Saint Laurent

There are many good and valid reasons why a salon should periodically update not only decor, but retail displays, lighting, furniture, and equipment. If your business décor is outdated, it may give clients a poor impression. A professional business image is very important to your clients, and remodeling tells clients that you understand this. A sharp looking business gives you credibility as an expert in personal appearance and presentation.

Periodic updates improve your clients' morale because they feel better about themselves just getting a great look in an up-to-date business environment. Remodeling also improves employee morale. A great looking business not only helps retain staff and lower turnover, it makes it easier to recruit new employees.

Color and fashion trends change approximately every five to seven years. To stay current, salons and spas should follow the same time frame. From a purely business point of view, you should remodel when business is declining or when new customers are not being generated.

Do not think of remodeling as simply painting or wallpapering. You need to keep your salon, retail area, equipment, and furniture up to date. Technological improvements are constantly being made on today's sleek, new equipment. Updated retail images are not only great improvements in a salon or spa, but add to the productivity of employees as well.

The continued offering of 5-star services doesn't stop with the service you provide, it must continue throughout the look of the entire salon. The importance of the upkeep of your salon's furnishings and common areas is essential. Listed below are a few things that you may not seem to notice in your salon that need to be looked at daily. If your salon's furnishings are starting to show some of these signs it's time for a salon makeover:

- Delamination or chipping of Formica on your front desk or any of your styling stations
- Drawers broken on front desk or styling stations
- Reception seating worn or stained from constant use
- Rust on the base of your styling chairs
- Tears or stains on the leather of your styling chairs
- Arms on styling chairs loose
- Pumps on styling chairs not working or leaking
- Mirrors on your styling stations losing their luster
- Retail shelving starting to sag
- Shampoo shuttles leaking or stained
- Roller carts or trays stained and drawers broken
- Color area stained and soiled
- Runny faucets on sinks
- Color of your furnishings outdated
- Bathroom vanities starting to peel or look like they need a coat of paint
- Loose seats on the toilets or miscolored
- Running faucets in the bathrooms
- Flooring showing signs of main traffic areas by being worn
- Ceiling tiles having water stains or loosing luster or sagging
- Finger prints on walls in main areas
- Color from treatments on the back of styling chairs

Remodeling Tips

Leslie McGwire, award-winning salon and spa designer, shares these tips for when you do remodel:

- Hiring a salon designer will assist you with major salon renovations, including the most current trends that are happening today.

- Colors and accents are just as important when remodeling your salon.

- Adding ornate trim in the right spots is an easy and inexpensive way to change appearance without spending a fortune.

- Painting is key to a quick fix-up when you can't go for a major redo.

- New flooring, although it can be expensive, is a great way to change the entire look of a salon.

- Color labs are hot, and if you have space they are a great way to enhance the look of your salon.

- Dry bars are also hot, and a great way to add a revenue stream to your salon—get on board now.

The importance of the upkeep of your salon is crucial in many ways. It's not only the customer experience we have to be concerned about. Yes, it's the biggest factor and we should always be concerned about how the customer sees the salon as a whole, but you must also realize as an owner or manager that the employees are essential to the success of your business, and an updated salon is good for employee morale. A happy employee makes for a happy customer and thus makes the whole experience better for all, including you as the owner.

CHAPTER 8

Front Desk Greatness

"Good design is good business."

– Thomas J. Watson

Many owners don't grasp the importance of the front desk in their salon or spa. One of the most important elements of designing your salon for beauty, profit, maximum efficiency, and quality service is left on the design table. The reasons are endless, but most of the time it comes down to budgeting and the importance of other areas of the salon usually wins. The main design emphasis is, and should be, on the styling area, color area and utility rooms. All are very important to the salon, but if you want to offer a 5-star salon atmosphere, you have to start at the front desk. It is, after all, often the first impression, the last impression, and the lasting impression.

Design for the 5-Star Experience

In design, "form follows function". Nothing can be truer than when designing reception desks for a salon or spa. Reception desks set the stage for the level of professionalism and the overall concept of the business. Not only should they be beautiful, but functional as well. Salons and spas, in particular, require their reception desks to be able to perform multiple tasks. They are the main command center of the entire salon. They must greet clients, perform transactions, and make new appointments. They must be sized properly too. If a desk is too large it will overwhelm the area, if too small it looks out of place and not well thought out. This can reflect negatively on the business as well.

Designing a desk that meets all this criteria will help create a reception area that has a memorable and inviting first impression.

Functionality

Desks that function well help the staff to be efficient and more willing to help clients in a friendly helpful manner. Remember when a guest new or old walks into the salon, although they may have been there before, they are no longer in their element. The salon or spa is foreign territory. The front desk is their focal point and usually takes the sting out of feeling out of place. The more welcoming the front desk, the more at home your guests will feel. If the front desk is big and clumsy and the client can't see the receptionist or feels intimidated, then you have lost the 5-star experience you are trying to create. Most of the time bigger is not better. More intimate usually wins every time.

An important question to ask when first designing a desk is how many people will be working behind the desk. This affects the length of the desk along with how many work stations the desk is to have. Works stations consist of an area for a monitor, keyboard, and computer. These stations must be ergonomically designed for optimal comfort. There are systems that can be added to help with organization too such as pigeon slots, cord management, and grommets and chases for other electrical wires. Various cabinet and drawer configurations can also be considered. It's important to make a list of all items that are used at the desk so that you can have a place for everything and everything in its place.

Another point to consider is if you'd like the receptionists to be at stand-up height or sit-down height. A stand-up desk has a higher receptionist's work counter and offers the ability to greet the clients eye to eye as they enter the salon. It also makes the receptionist more willing to get involved with the retail sales. They are ready to assist a client with questions about a certain product or service and may be more apt to get the client coffee and hang a coat it they are already in a standing position.

ADA compliancy is also a very important feature of a functional desk. This is achieved by having varying desk heights so handicapped clients and employees can have easy access to the desk and transaction counter. ADA counter height is usually between 29" and 34" high. It's fun to be creative with this element by interjecting various materials on the face of the desk along with varying depths to help achieve a look that is interesting and inviting to all.

Look

The look of a reception desk is probably the element that gets noticed the most. It's important for the design to be consistent with the overall concept of the salon. All too often people purchase a stock reception desk from a local business store just to save a few dollars. This does nothing for the design of the space and makes the salon look temporary, unprofessional and sloppy. With good design comes great business. You want a desk that reflects your talent and ambition. Whether it's traditional elements, with crown and rosette moldings, stream-lined with metal accents and minimalist lines, or more boutique-like with an upholstered tufted face, it's important to mirror the overall concept of the salon or spa.

One of my favorite design elements is using acrylic panels and illuminating them from behind. It gives a unique look to the salon by day and looks even better at night. Passersby will notice the glowing desk and be curious to stop in for a visit. Top surfaces have many options too. Granite, Corian, quartz, glass, metal all help to give the desk pizzazz! These same surfaces can be used on the face of the desk. Laminate is one of the most popular and least expensive surfaces. It is extremely versatile and comes in thousands of colors along with rich wood grains of all different shades and species.

Designing a reception desk is a process that should be well thought out. One option is to seek out a salon design professional for assistance. They offer a plethora of design advice and options, all within various set budgets. This will ensure that your reception desk creates the first impression you intend it to have, not only aesthetically but functionally as well.

First Impressions: The Look of the Salon

★ Your customers' first impression of your salon is important - make it count.

★ Negative little problems can add up to big problems while positive little touches can add up to spectacular.

★ A clean salon and sharp-looking staff is fundamental to a good impression.

★ Make sure your salon décor is not outdated, dull, or in disrepair.

★ A great front desk can make a great first, last, and lasting impression.

PART III

Good Customer Communications in the Salon

CHAPTER 9

It Starts With the Greeting

"You had me at 'Hello'."
– from *Jerry McGuire*

When guests come to your home, you greet them, don't you? If you are in the shower, you grab a robe and run to the door; if you are doing home chores or conducting an important business call, you stop what you are doing and go to the front door of your home to greet your guests.

No matter what you're doing, your guests are your focus and answering your door to greet them is a top priority. You give them a big handshake, hug, hello, or hi there; if they are a friend you use their first name and you may invite them in. Your guest is your priority and you focus all your attention on him or her. If you were to time this greeting, the whole process would be less than a minute, maybe 30 seconds.

How many times have you entered a place of business and it felt like hell had frozen over before someone even acknowledged your presence? No big hello, nice to see you, great to have you back again, have you been here before, we're so happy you've arrived - not even a hand gesture, simply nothing. You seat yourself and wait for someone, anyone, to acknowledge your presence. No matter what type of business, you already have a bad taste for the experience you are about to encounter. It doesn't matter how good things get from this point on, your service didn't start as a 5-star experience.

Greet Your Customers Promptly

A business study clocked the number of seconds people had to wait to be greeted in several businesses. Researchers asked customers how long they had been waiting before someone acknowledged their presence. In every case, the customers' estimate of time elapsed was much longer than the actual time. A customer waiting 30 or 40 seconds often feels like it's been three or four minutes. Time drags when you're waiting to be noticed and you know you're going to be paying for a service.

In today's world we live in an era of instant gratification. People want what they want, and they want it now. "ASAP" has become our standard deadline as a society, and when it comes to serving customers and offering a 5-star service level, your greeting had better be fast, polite, and right on target.

In face-to-face interactions, a prompt greeting reduces customer stress. Throw in the customer's first and/or last name, smile, and put out your hand for a handshake, and the whole world just stopped and said you are important and we appreciate your business. Why would customers feel stress when entering a place of business? Remember, whether they have been there before or this is their first visit, they are not on their own turf and are likely to feel somewhat uncomfortable. The anticipation of the service, new treatment, new color or hairstyle has them in a bit of a tizzy, giving them a hurry-up-and-get-this-going or get-me-out-of-here attitude. Remember, ASAP is the new norm.

A quick, friendly greeting starts to relax the customer and greases the wheels of smooth service.

Speak Up and Shout It Out!

Who is the designated person in your salon or spa to greet your customers? Is it your front desk person? Your entire staff, if they are near the front entrance? Is it the manager or maybe you, the owner? I suggest that it should be everyone who has the capability to smile, put their hand out and say hello. That's right – everyone from the front desk person to the girl or guy who shampoos hair. If they can walk and talk, they can certainly acknowledge a customer and show that your establishment is ready to serve. 5-star service doesn't stop if the salon greeter is not at her post the moment a customer enters. If you want to offer 5-star service, it starts at the top – with you – and it trickles down to every member of your staff.

How many times have you walked into the fast food restaurant Moe's and heard "WELCOME to MOE'S!"? It's not a whisper, you don't have to guess what they're saying and you certainly know it's meant for you. It's not the person closest to the door who shouts it out, it's the entire staff. It's the teamwork approach to 5-star service.

Verbally greet a customer within ten seconds of the time he or she comes into your place of business. It will take a customer that long to put away their car keys and cell phone and acclimate to the area. The clock starts ticking as soon as that front door swings open, and your entire staff needs to be cognizant that a guest has arrived.

It doesn't matter whether you are busy with another customer or on a phone call, you must pause to say hello, make eye contact, make sure you have a big smile on your face no matter how bad your day may be going, and let them know you'll be ready to help them soon. If you cannot greet them immediately, your smile should compensate for this and buy you a few seconds.

Let's look at a quick example of what might happen in a salon that could cause you, one of your staff, or your receptionist to not offer that 5-star greeting experience.

Example - Mary the shopper has picked out three retail products, and she's asking you how the products were made, are they organic, and what can she expect from using them? She has quickly thrown off your normal routine at the front desk. The phone is ringing and you have two other guests waiting patiently to pay for their services. OMG, what else can happen? The inevitable of course - the front door of the salon swings open, and in walks what appears to be a new customer. He walks in, notices a crowd and immediately feels out of place. Remember what we said earlier in this chapter: clients are not on their home turf, and entering your salon or spa is like walking into a new world. The clock has already started ticking and you have less than ten seconds to make 5-star service happen. It's up to you, your staff and/ or anyone else to step it up, remember your 5-star philosophies, and make things right.

Okay, do you throw up your hands and have your entire staff yell "WELCOME to MOE'S!"? Don't think so. However, your receptionist can turn to the guest she is working with and simply say, "Excuse me, I'll be right back," stop what she is doing, and immediately address the new guest. Explain that things are a tad bit busy and promise that in a minute or two she will assist with getting them situated. She then looks for any person in the salon or spa to assist until she regains control of the reception area. Together they can continue to try their best to make everyone happy - never losing their cool and always with the perpetual smile that never goes away no matter how bad things get. Job well done! 5-star service still managed to happen, although for a minute or two it seemed like the world was coming to an end and all was lost.

The receptionist and/or greeter must at least acknowledge your customers no matter how busy you are. Letting a customer know you are busy with a simple "I'll be with you in a minute" - said with a big smile - goes a long way and can save a customer from turning around and walking out the door.

More Than Hello

When you do have time to properly greet your customer, it should be more than "Hello." You should always greet them by name. A front desk professional knows a client is coming in at a certain time. The appointment is on her computer or logged into the appointment book. How nice to be greeted with, "Good morning, Mrs. Client! It's so nice to see you again. We are looking forward to taking care of you today."

But don't stop there with your greeting. If you really want to provide 5-star service, go the extra mile in your welcome. Offer to take their coat or point out where the hangers/hooks are; offer to take the wet umbrella. Ask if they would like anything to drink - coffee, water or a glass of wine? Most clients will decline your friendly offer, but will still be impressed you asked.

Talk With Your Eyes

The writer Samuel Richardson once said, "Where words are restrained, the eyes often talk a great deal." How many times have you acknowledged or had someone get your attention with their eyes? The eyes are a great way to say hello - aloud - without talking. Eye contact will buy you a few seconds when an approaching customer is looking for assistance. Simply looking at your customer tells them much about your willingness to serve.

As with your greeting, your timing is important. The ten-second rule applies here as well, even if you are busy with another person. Quicker is better. The good thing about eye contact is that all you have to do is look up, smile, and let the customer know you see them. Bow your head and look straight in their eyes. Job well done! They know you see them.

Eye contact creates a bond between you and your customers. It conveys your interest in communicating further. It builds rapport. You don't have to interrupt what you are doing with another customer. Using your eyes allows you to multitask while still giving ultimate service no matter how busy you may be. Just a pause and a quick look will oblige a customer to deal with you further, greatly reducing the chance they'll feel ignored and leave.

Smiling Says a Thousand Words

How many times have you walked into a place of business and the person who greets you has a sour look on their face? Certainly not the welcoming smile we all would prefer. You immediately think something is wrong and maybe you should leave and come back, walk outside, or snap your fingers and pray that this person is no longer there. We have all experienced an unhappy employee who ruins our visit. Most of the time, we don't come back if we don't have to.

How hard is it to put a smile on your face? It really doesn't require much. You don't have to eat something that makes you smile (although eating something good does put a smile on your face!) You don't have to go to the gym every day to produce a smile. So why is it so hard to smile when a customer walks in the front door of your salon? Guess what, salon owners, managers and employees - it's not hard. Smiles should be mandatory in your salon or spa.

If someone can't smile, then have your makeup artist airbrush a smile on that person's face! Seriously, I hope you get what I am saying here. If they don't like smiling then they shouldn't be working for you in the service business. Here's a bit of business advice: send the non-smiling employee down the street to your competitor and have them work there. You will surely get some of their customers in no time flat.

Smiling tells customers that they came to the right place and they are on friendly ground. Remember what we said before: customers get weird when they are not on familiar turf. Smiling puts them at ease and lets them know they are on friendly ground. Smile with your eyes and your mouth. Let your face show that you're glad your guest arrived. Remember, you are not fully dressed for customer service work unless you have a smile on your face.

Rocket Science or Common Sense

When you went into the salon or spa business, you knew you had the creativity and business sense to do it, but you may not have realized how important the service offering is to the success of your business. What we have discussed in this chapter is not rocket science; it is the common sense basics that you must apply to your 5-star business strategy. How many salons or spas lose their business edge by not putting in the little things that are so important? The cost to implement the basic principles we've discussed is nothing.

The greeting is the first part of your service offering. You need to make it memorable. Simply saying hello, giving a handshake or a hug when appropriate, using the client's name, and smiling and looking in the customer's eyes is basic Business 101. I may not be a Rhodes Scholar, but my Mom and Dad taught me most of these things when I was a youngster. Saying hello, smiling when you meet someone new, and putting out a hand as a gesture of kindness were not invented yesterday. You must use these basic principles of kindness in your salon or spa no matter what service level you are trying to reach. Since 5-star service is what your business is striving for, then hone in on these basic skills and make sure each and every one of your employees uses them when meeting, greeting, and servicing your valued customers.

CHAPTER 10

It Continues Throughout the Visit

"I've learned that people will forget what you said, people will forget what you did, but people will never forget how you made them feel."

– Maya Angelou

You can do everything imaginable to create a top-notch salon, but this will not guarantee that your clients are happy and that you will make them feel important. Many of us forget to think about our clients and their feelings when we are so wrapped up in our own.

All of us want to feel as though we matter. Think about the last time someone went out of their way to make you feel special. I'll bet you can clearly remember what you felt like, what you needed, and how that person made your day by doing something special for you. The point is, we remember when someone goes out of their way to make us feel special. It can be a very small gesture, but it creates a bond between the giver and the receiver. Whatever it is, we are sure to remember it and talk about it. It makes us go out of our way to be around that person or their place of business. People gravitate to those who make them feel special. Making someone feel special starts with good communication.

Acknowledge

We all have experienced waiting in line for something. Most of the time, we have gone out of our way to be at a specific place at a specific time. Has anyone ever said they are sorry for making you wait? When you go unnoticed, you feel that your time is not valued.

Your clients' time is valuable too. They have families like you and they have put forth some effort to make it on time to their appointment with you. When a client is sitting there in the waiting area, her stylist should acknowledge her. This is especially important if she has been waiting longer than usual. Walk over and smile and say hello. Shake her hand or give her a hug, apologize for the delay. These small things minimize the fact that you are running late. Remember a time when you were ignored—you don't want your client to experience that and develop bad feelings about you or your salon.

Listen

Once they're in your chair, the most important part of your communication may not be what you say, but how you listen. How many times has someone said to you, "Are you listening to me?" Maybe it's your children, spouse, or clients. Most people can tell when you are listening to them and when your mind is somewhere else. It makes people feel important when you give them 100 percent of your attention and really listen to what they are saying.

Your customer may be going through an illness, a divorce, or work-related problems. Listening to their stories is important to them because true listening in today's world is rare. Sometimes you might feel more like a counselor than a hairstylist. If you are developing a close bond with your client, they will share their good and bad news. A shoulder to cry on is part of the job and part of the service you provide. If you have to apply a hair color or give a haircut, why not pay attention to your client at the same time? If it makes them feel good, go out of your way to be a good listener.

Training your salon team to become good listeners is very important too. They are representing your company. It's not just the personal story you have to listen to, but the service your client is asking for. You want to make sure your team is applying the exact color or giving the hairstyle the client asks for.

Explain

One of the most important communication basics that many salon businesses tend to forget is that many times the service technician doesn't communicate what he or she is doing or will be doing during the service. On a spa vacation, I experienced a perfect example of top-notch, 5-star-level communication from each spa employee I encountered.

The receptionist (who was really much more than her title) approached me three times within a ten-minute timeframe to explain that I had come in early and that the massage therapist was preparing the room for my service. Not only did she explain in detail that the service provider was changing sheets and disinfecting the room for a more refreshing treatment, she described the candles that would be used and asked what type of music I preferred. (She was also soft selling me for the checkout, because both the candles and music could be purchased at the front desk. At this point I was so overwhelmed with her 5-star customer service, I had no idea what she had quietly accomplished.)

The receptionist also explained where I would be changing, described the locker area and said that there was a male technician waiting to walk me to my locker and changing area. She asked me what type of massage I preferred: soft, Swedish, and so on. She would forward this information to the massage therapist and would close the door to eliminate any confusion.

In this example, the communication level was exceptional. Every single person working in your salon or spa should be able to communicate clearly with customers, both verbally and in writing. Clarity is the essence of communication; when you're clear on what you are doing for a customer there is no room for misunderstanding or error. One of the most important communication basics that many companies forget is that it's not enough just to convey important information; you need to convey it consistently and in a timely fashion.

Apologize

Don't think your salon and staff will never run into problems. With so many variables, it seems that something could go wrong at any time—personality clashes, chemicals being mixed incorrectly or spilled, misbehaving or dull scissors, electrical equipment failure, and plumbing or hot water issues. In fact, you might think, "How is it that more bad things don't happen in a given day?" When things do go wrong, make sure you and your staff simply say, "We are sorry." An apology goes a long way. It is a simple way to build a loyal client. The better person always apologizes first; don't let your ego get in the way. You may also have to be prepared to give a full refund or cover the service for the day at no charge to the client. This will depend on the mishap that occurred, but you should be ready for this or other recovery gifts in the event that something goes wrong.

Thank

The easiest way to make any client feel good and appreciated is to say, "Thank you!" It doesn't cost you a thing to show how much you appreciate the fact that you have loyal customers who keep coming back to your salon. How many times have you forgotten to say thank you?

The last chapter talked about the importance of how you greet your customers. It is just as important to say goodbye and thank you, again using their name as you close out their service and visit for the day. Both the provider, upon completing the service, and the receptionist, as they're checking the client out, should say thank you.

The following has worked for over 25 years, "Thank you for your business, Mrs. Client. As always, it is a pleasure having you at my salon. Your continued business is appreciated by me and my family as well."

All of us should implement these practices of acknowledging, listening, explaining, apologizing when necessary, and thanking our customers every day. When we do, it will make our work more enjoyable and create a strong legion of clients who leave feeling good and who will continue to support our business.

CHAPTER 11

Salon Talk

*"We thought we had the answers, it was the
questions we had wrong."*

— Bono

We all assume that our clients understand the salon language we use daily—the language we use to communicate with other salon team members when mixing a color or reaching for a bottle of shampoo. If you are having a conversation with your product distributor about color techniques and how to apply a new keratin-related product, you're talking salon talk and both of you get it, but the conversation you have with your client has to be quite different.

Client communication, or let's call it plain old talking, should be the easiest thing in the world. But often you're saying, "Let's add some depth with lowlights," and she's hearing "blah, blah, blah." Or "I think your hair is flat and may need a bit of texture." What does that mean to your client? To many, you may as well be a duck quacking in their ear. It really sounds good and shows you know what you're talking about, but does your client understand what it means? If you're not sure, then your communication isn't working. Here are ten ways to eliminate the static and make sure you're coming through loud and clear.

Clear Channel

Stop on the way home from the salon, pick up a pack of Q-tips, and start swabbing. Clean out the cobwebs and ear wax. Now you have no excuses for not hearing what your customer is saying. The first step toward being a better communicator is learning how to listen. Make it your mission to find out what is important to your client. One of the best ways to get people talking is by asking open-ended questions. "What are your goals with your hair?" "If I gave you the scissors, what would you do?" "What would you like to see done differently?" "Have you seen a style on TV or in a magazine you like or would like to wear?" Once you've established that you're genuinely interested in what a client has to say, get ready for an earful.

Hand Signals

A prominent stylist told me, "Don't jump in and start touching the hair right away, this blocks communication by limiting and scaring off the client." Instead, let her do it herself. Encourage her to pick up that curl that never falls quite where she'd like, or that highlight that makes her feel all Cruella Deville. In addition to noting the problem areas she points out, study how she actually touches her hair, how she combs and brushes it and what she does to get out the door in the morning. Sometimes you will see right away that someone is just too timid in how she handles her hair, which keeps her from styling it correctly and may be part of her problem. So, keep your hands off, and your services will be right on.

Un-Fuzz Buzzwords

Everyone understands what highlights are, but you need to explain the meaning behind trendier terms. Remember the confusion between "surfer" and "skater" cuts that had stylists wiping out a few years ago? To stay on the same wavelength, discuss the definition of a term together before the scissors come out of the case. But it isn't just the newest salon slang that can be mystifying. Even "soft" and "wispy" mean different things to different people. "Layers" have been re-dubbed "invisible layers," so clients who have been traumatized by overly exuberant Farrah-phile stylists won't be afraid to try the technique a second time.

Get to the Point

Once you're clear on the terminology, explain why you think a particular technique would work for that client. Demystify it. Share how each aspect of the style lines up with your client's goals. Echo what she told you when you first asked her what she wanted for her hair. That means linking the cut to everything from her face shape to her desire to save time. We call it "reviewing the benefits." Here's what she would say to a 100% gray client who wants to look younger without spending a lot of time at the salon: "I'm using color with a brown base. It has some warmth, which is necessary to cover gray, and will also flatter your skin tone. And with this particular formulation, you won't have to worry about fading as long as you come in for a refresher every six weeks."

Show and Tell

Before the first no-turning-back snip is made, use the comb or scissors to clarify things like angle and length. For example, hold the comb up to the side of your client's head and tilt it at the same slant you plan to create in your design line. It may be a good idea to pivot the comb at the top of the head to show the direction of the cut. After you've finished your slicing and pointing, demonstrate how to style the hair—but don't actually apply any mousse or gel. Let the client watch and absorb what you're doing, and then try it herself. Coach her, so she has a better chance of recreating the look at home.

Sign Language

Ask any Italian—you can say a lot with your hands. Don't be afraid to use them in place of your tools when showing a client her options for shape and line. You'll also learn a lot about the condition of the hair as you move it around. To show that slicing doesn't mean losing length, use your hand to illustrate. Hold it out, and tell the client to think of the fingers as sections of hair. Then bend down the ring or middle finger, leaving the others extended. This clearly shows that with slicing, a client will still retain length, but lose some of the weight that's keeping her hair from being as lively as she'd like.

Eye Contact

Avoid that superior hairdresser stance, looking down from above. Have you ever explained a story for what seemed like ten minutes and your audience just looked at you in a fog? You know they didn't listen and if you asked them to repeat the story I am sure they couldn't. Don't be that person. In order to truly understand what your client is saying and explaining, you must face the client and look in their eyes. This may be a bit weird, but I guarantee you will get what they are trying to communicate to you. Another good way to communicate better is to have rolling chairs for stylists, which can be easily wheeled around to face clients. For the consultation, always look the person in the eye. If you're tired and you feel your ADD kicking in, put your hand on top of the client's. Touching is a way to ensure you are listening—plus, your client may find it a bit awkward and get right to the point. Win-win for both of you. Once you've moved on to describing the actual cut, go ahead and stand behind the chair again, so your client can look in the mirror as you explain what you plan to do. But return to face-to-face mode when you're discussing how to use that new pomade or serum. Always let the client know she ultimately has veto power to decide whether to go with one of your suggestions. Making eye contact helps establish that you have equal roles.

Gab Fest

Once you've made all the technical details clear, get back to the personal. Clients keep coming back to you because of the relationship the two of you share. Again, you can ask open-ended questions, so people can reveal as much or as little about their beyond-the-salon lives as they want. You may get soap opera-level detail, or just a few choice tidbits. Show interest, without being pushy. I find that a stylist who uses their client's name frequently during the service adds to the friendly feeling. There is a reason the Ritz Carlton uses people's first and last name throughout the entire stay at their hotels. Dropping the customer name over and over through their service shows that you respect them, and want them back. If you're shy, or worried that the conversation might distract you and lead to errors—just talk about what you're doing. You can't go wrong discussing the process. It will impress the client, and put you at ease.

Memorize Lines

Sometimes there is so much we want to share with clients that we don't realize we've forgotten to mention something until we switch off the blow dryer. Since you can't install a teleprompter at your station, create a script for yourself. You don't need to buy screenwriting software. Just jotting down key ideas on index cards helps. For those off-days, write down some reminders of things to discuss while working on clients. We suggest including buzzwords and their definitions, questions to ask, and objectives you'd like to meet. Another crib sheet: the Redken Consultation Pad, used at Hair Cuttery. It lists all the company's products, and you check off the ones you prescribe for a client. She takes it to the retail area and stocks up.

Money Talks

Even if you've communicated so well that your client gets precisely the gorgeous look she wanted, sticker shock at the reception desk can put her in an ugly mood. The price of a cut should flatter her wallet, not just the shape of her face. People don't like to ask how much things cost. So during the consultation, make it easy for them to stay in their price range by discussing dollars. 5-star service means always including your client in what is going on. If you are great at upselling, always and I do mean always, explain what the added service or product purchase will add to their bill. A clever way to handle this is by asking the client, "How much did you budget for your hair today?" This helps determine what services you should offer and what products to suggest. Someone who wants to spend $100 won't be getting a hair straightening treatment, but she might opt for some new smoothing products.

CHAPTER 12

Dealing With & Resolving Conflict

"I never said it would be easy. I only said it would be worth it."

– Mae West

In our day-to-day life within our salons and spas we are faced with handling and resolving conflict. Conflict is unfortunately a natural part of any business or part of life, whether it's dealing with internal customers (your salon/spa team) or external customers (your salon/spa guests). Conflict is brought on by different expectations and by our different beliefs, diverse backgrounds, life experiences, and values.

In our roles as salon owners, managers, or team leaders, we must have an effective system in place to deal with sticky situations and conflicts when they arise. Internal conflicts between team members can be just as bad as conflicts with customers; they can create a tense environment and be destructive to the entire team. If we manage conflict in the wrong way, a simple challenge can spiral out of control, cooperation can break down and your team mission and vision may be threatened. Teach your entire team how to resolve conflict and set expectations in place so that there is no room for ongoing conflict in your salon. In order to resolve conflict, it helps to take a positive approach.

- **Handle conflicts in a timely manner** - It's likely the problem will not just go away. The challenge may get worse with time. Nip it in the bud as soon as possible.

- **Invite the other person to talk about the situation first** - "Seek first to understand, then to be understood." In other words, let the other person go first. Communication is a critical part of conflict resolution.

- **Listen with intent to truly hear** - When listening, you must approach the conversation with one intention: to thoroughly hear the other person's point of view. Follow up with statements such as, "I understand how you feel," or "Help me understand why …"

- **Apologize** - Apologize for your part in the conflict. By apologizing, you're not accepting the entire blame; however, you are taking responsibility for your part in it. Use statements like, "I am sorry you feel that way," or "I apologize for …"

- **Develop a plan of action** - Remember, no one wins! Discuss what would be a positive outcome. Develop several choices that would meet the overall objective. We all like choices.

Whether the conflict is with your staff or a salon guest, the end result is to get everyone back on track as quickly as possible with as little discomfort as possible.

Keeping Customer Complaints from Becoming a Major Crisis

No one likes to receive a complaint from a customer— but complaints are worth their weight in gold if an organization learns from them and then uses the information to improve the customer experience. Customer complaints can be used to build a better customer experience and turn an unsatisfied customer into a raving fan. How your salon team handles the crisis will determine if your salon offers 5-star services or handles conflicts the way your competitor down the street does: poorly.

The key is for the service provider to immediately take action. Make sure that he or she asks what would make the customer happy and then verify before taking any action. Customers will rarely ask for more that we are prepared to offer, so ask what will make them happy first. Once they have made their suggestions, then verify that if you are able to provide that remedy, the customer will be satisfied. Nothing worse than working to resolve an issue only to find that the customer is still not happy.

Move quickly to resolution. Once a resolution is agreed, move quickly. In fact, a good recovery builds greater customer loyalty than simply delivering as expected — so make sure to use this to your advantage. The exact opposite is true, however, if the customer is "given the runaround" by being transferred from employee to manager to higher level executive before their problem is handled. There is nothing worse than a scorned customer unhappy with a cut or color. A bad woman's haircut lasts at least 6 to 8 weeks. That's a long time for someone to fester about how poorly they look and how bad the customer service was at your salon. The worst part is this customer can quickly go to the airwaves and start an onslaught of negative publicity on Facebook, Yelp, Twitter and more about your salon, her service and how poorly she was treated. Ouch!

Provide the tools needed to resolve a salon crisis. Give employees options when dealing with difficult customers or those with an issue the employee can't resolve. Encourage your team to take charge if a crisis does arise. For example, if a customer bought an item on clearance, and the store's policy is to never accept returns on clearance items, allow employees to offer the customer a complimentary gift card, a new product worth the same as the item purchased, or a service reduction equal to the product purchased. While it may not be exactly what the customer asks for, it will show customer appreciation and help them see that the company is going out of its way to satisfy the complaint.

Empower employees to handle customer complaints themselves. Obviously, there will be a point when a more senior person must make a decision in dealing with a complaint, but empowering employees to deal with common complaints and issues on their own will go a long way toward creating a more positive customer experience and increasing employee engagement. It also helps when a manager or the owner of the salon steps in to see how they can also help to resolve a crisis. Team work is a good approach to helping resolve an issue. It also shows the customer that everyone is interested in resolving an issue and gives the perception of how valuable that customer is.

There will be times when nothing can be done to satisfy an unhappy customer. At that point, the service provider must simply defer that customer to a manager or the salon's owner. Service providers who handle customer service complaints quickly, efficiently and professionally will minimize those issues and will give employees a sense of ownership in their jobs and in the company.

The owner of the salon or manager must present the customer with a solution. Once you get past the screaming and yelling and inappropriate name calling (hopefully all on their part, not yours!), figuring out the right resolution takes a little thinking. Duck and cover is not a solution. The problem will not resolve itself. Provide a solution to create closure. However, before suggesting a solution, here is the sequential order of things to consider for creating the best resolution for your business.

1. **Determine the future worth of the customer.** Don't make the mistake of an inexperienced business owner by assuming the customer is always right or altering your attitude based on the flack they throw up in your face. All that is important at this point in time is to quickly assess the future worth of the customer.

2. **Ask the customer what they want to resolve the matter and if you accommodate them will they be happy.** The customer's response will indicate whether they are reasonable or not. This will then help you further determine the future worth of the customer. Are they making unrealistic demands? If so, chances are they are going to be more trouble than they're worth. And if not, it becomes easy for you to give them what they want – creating a more satisfying experience for them.

3. **Determine what it will cost you to resolve the matter to their liking.** Weigh the cost of the resolution against the future profits that they will bring you. If they are suggesting compensation that seems excessive, look at the bigger picture before you deny their demands. When considering what it will cost you, don't forget the cost of having an unhappy customer venting about your salon to their friends and online. Surveys indicate that people make decisions based on other people's recommendations more than listening to experts or pundits. Like it or not, customers are in control, and the best thing you can do is try to have them on your side. By losing some upfront money to compensate an unhappy client, you might not only win back this client, but you'll also help avoid the negative reviews of an unhappy customer.

You're not done yet. Presenting a solution is not the final step. Once the customer has been satisfied (or you are satisfied with the extent of your solution), there are two more steps to minimize the re-occurrence of the same issue and the loss to your business.

4. **Determine whether the customer was right or wrong.** Now is the time to assess the customer's perception. If the customer was wrong, consider what led to their perception and the possibility for other customers to come to the same conclusion. If the customer was right, giving them a solution is only a band aid. Dig down and find out the root of the problem.

5. **Implement a corrective action.** Create a corrective action to both cure the root problem and to implement a policy of how to handle similar situations in the future.

If you never have unhappy customers, chances are that you don't have very many customers. Whether the root of their ire is linked to a bad day or to a bad experience with you, being prepared with these quick steps will only benefit you by creating the best resolution for your business.

In the game of salon ownership there will be times the high stress of dealing with difficult customers dominated by the theatrical personalities of your styling team. Those times, you will have to step out of your outer body and go into embodiment of your Zen calm, able to keep your composure and grace in the gritty, chaotic world of salon employees and customers.

The key to your success will be your ability to handle problems effectively, by obtaining closure, and turning out the lights to any problems, respected by both your staff and customers because of the ease and elegance of how you handle things. This is a true master of 5-star service and salon ownership.

CHAPTER 13

How to Say "No"

"It takes a great deal of courage to stand up to your enemies, but even more to stand up to your friends."

— J.K. Rowling

Finding and retaining customers is your most critical task as a salon owner. Offering 5-star service is crucial to your success, but when it comes to saying no to a customer request, it takes special skills and a trained staff to effectively maintain composure and keep your client satisfied.

The last thing you want to do after bringing in a new client is lose them. It is difficult enough to retain the customers you have. As a business owner, you have very little room to say no to a customer - to refuse them when they ask for new features, services you don't offer, reduced prices, or the most ridiculous, bizarre haircut or color ever. Let's face it, people can be rude at times and their requests outlandish. The way you treat them during this time is crucial to maintaining your salon's 5-star service atmosphere.

For generations in the customer service business, we've been told, "The customer is always right." This business philosophy is so ingrained in us that we feel we should never deviate from it. After all, "right" customers are satisfied customers and customer satisfaction distinguishes one business or service provider in a sea of intense competition, especially in the beauty industry. Client satisfaction should be priority one for any successful salon owner.

However, there will come a time when a customer pushes you or one of your staff too much or when you are backed into a corner and something has to give. You know what your customer is asking is extreme and wrong, and in this case you do have to say no. Saying no at some point in our careers is inevitable. You cannot honor every request that your customers make. You do not have unlimited time and endless resources to fulfill their every desire. But you never know how the customer will react and you certainly don't want to lose a customer's loyalty, much less their business. However, and this is a big however, you also don't want to lose your reputation!

As an example, let's look at Britney Spears' famous haircut situation. Suppose she is your customer and asks you, her trusted hairstylist, to shave her head. What should you do? Unless she is starring in a movie that requires a shaved head, obviously the decision should be to say no. None of us would want to lose a top celebrity such as Britney as a customer, but would you want to be known as the person who actually cut and shaved her head?

Saying No the Right Way

When the time comes that you are faced with saying no to your client you want to be fully prepared. Your response will depend on the customer, how long you have had a relationship and what type of relationship you have. You will approach each no situation differently. The following tips will help you successfully handle the inevitable no.

- Always look the customer directly in the eyes when saying no.
- Force yourself to smile or laugh—this will put some positive energy on an awkward situation.
- Actively listen to the customer while they explain in detail why you should do what they are requesting.
- Only talk in a low voice. Do not raise your voice at all, no matter how frustrated you may be.
- Explain in detail why you will not do what they are requesting and why you said no.
- If they continue to badger you, listen intently and then say no again.
- Always say no politely.
- Never use profanity, regardless of how upset you or your customer may be.
- Stick to one thing and do not change the subject, no matter what.

- Try to resolve the issue regardless of how difficult it may be.

- Always say thank you and that you appreciate their business, regardless of the outcome.

- Reach out to your boss or manager for help if the situation becomes tense.

Turn a Negative into a Positive

The top producers in any field, whether it's Wall Street, sales or the beauty industry, are problem solvers. These top dogs find a diplomatic way to turn a negative situation into a positive without affecting the relationship with the customer. You, too, can turn a no into a positive solution using finesse and negotiating skills. Here are a few examples.

- Help your customer understand what they are actually asking, and how they can better achieve it or do without it.

- If the request is reasonable (for example, for a service you don't provide), consider referring them to a non-competitor that does provide that service (such as a spa that does waxing but not hair).

- Explain how a bad hair color choice or haircut will not flatter their face or skin color. If you can do so sincerely, compliment them while doing this ("You have such a beautiful complexion but this color just won't complement it.")

- Explain that doing something for the moment lasts a lot longer than the moment. If they are still adamant, you could recommend they try a temporary solution such as rinse-out color before they do something more drastic.

- If they ask you to do something unethical, explain you are in this business for the long haul and cannot do anything to violate your code of ethics, so you will not tolerate the request. This shows your customer that you are a good, ethical person. The next time they come in, they will not ask you to do anything that they know deep down will violate your standards of conduct.

Rome Wasn't Built in a Day

If you don't say no when you should because you're worried a customer might leave, then you may be missing the big picture on how you will grow your book of business.

It takes time to develop key relationships with customers. None of the top stylists in the country grew their reputations and book of business overnight. These relationships were built over years by bringing quality work and valuable solutions to their customers. If a customer request doesn't make sense and you tell them no, a good customer will understand this and respect you for it. If you stand up and say no, it shows you have confidence in yourself and the expertise to make good decisions for both you and your customer. That, of course, doesn't mean you should say no a lot. "The customer is almost always right" is still a great philosophy. If you don't think the cut or color they're asking for will be as flattering as their current style, but it's not a drastic mistake, give them what they want.

Let Them Go

When you have to say no, do it and don't worry yourself over it; move on and stay focused on the big picture. If your customer continues to ask you to do things out of the ordinary and you find that you are in a constant battle to keep them happy, let them go elsewhere. Your competitors will be equally challenged by this customer. Customers like this may never be happy, and may find themselves roaming between salons never achieving satisfaction.

They will probably find someone somewhere that will fulfill their request, but better they be seen walking out of that salon! Saying no is difficult in the short-term, but sometimes you're better off in the long-term.

PART III - SUMMARY

Good Customer Communications in the Salon

★ Get off on the right foot by greeting your customers promptly and personally.

★ Continue great communication throughout their visit by listening to your customers, explaining what you're doing and always thanking them for their business.

★ Make sure your salon talk is at the customer's level so they understand and are comfortable with everything you're doing.

★ Conflicts will arise, both among your staff and with customers … deal with them quickly and effectively.

★ Saying "no" may be the right answer sometimes.

PART IV

Communication With Customers Outside the Salon

CHAPTER 14

Branding Your Salon

"A product can be quickly outdated, but a successful brand is timeless."

– Stephen King

Y ou are in large part responsible for your guests image and self-esteem. You are also responsible for your own image. Your brand is the cornerstone of your reputation. Your brand consists of a color scheme, image, graphics, and logo. Think about your favorite brands. What feelings and memories come to you when you see their image and logo in marketing materials? You want to create a brand that your guests associate with the feelings they have while they are in your salon. If your salon is a relaxing salon and day spa, you want your brand to reflect calm and relaxation. If your salon is high energy, then your brand should reflect that feeling.

Your brand should be consistent across all mediums: the signs in your window, the color of your walls, the background of your website, your menu, your Facebook page, your Google Places listing, and so on. Brand awareness is what you get when someone has an emotional reaction or memory (hopefully a positive one) when they see your image. When your guest gets an email from you, they should be transported to the feeling they get when they are in the salon to visit you. Consistency and repetition are the keys. Your goal is to be top-of-mind for your guests whenever possible, and having a strong brand will help you do that.

Branding is helping your customers understand what it is that your business offers. The first thing that pops in their mind for hair or spa related treatments should be your salon or spa. Think about that for a minute. What's the best way to get this to stick in their head whenever they are brushing their hair, applying makeup, showering and using the shampoo and conditioners your business sells.

This mind-altering brand builder can simply be a catchy phrase in your salon's name or a cool symbol on your logo. Let's go back in time and think about the barber's pole in front of the barbershop. Every man knew exactly what was going on in that storefront and never really had to think about where to go for a haircut. This made it easy for men to relate the barber pole to getting a haircut, no matter where they were in any town or city. Genius, and so easy to understand.

Branding should come easy once you truly get a firm understanding on how you want your business to be perceived. The simpler, the better; if you make it difficult for people to understand your brand, then you will blend in with everyone else around you.

CHAPTER 15

Contacting Your Customers

"My belief is that communication is the best way to create strong relationships."

— Jada Pinkett Smith

Y ou must communicate with your customers when they are not in the salon in order to keep your brand top-of-mind, so that the next time they do need a service they will think of your salon. You have to decide how you're going to contact your customers and then be consistent. You can choose to communicate with your guests with notes sent through the mail, but you may find that stamps and the amount of time it takes to prepare these types of communications are too costly. Phone calls are an option that can be less expensive, but they are more labor intense and potentially more intrusive to the guest. You will also probably find that you usually get voice mail when using this method of contacting customers, which is not the response you are looking for. Electronic communications are a more time- and expense-efficient method of getting in touch with your guests. Since over 80% of adult Americans have email addresses, you may find that your guests prefer electronic communications.

Getting to Know Your Customer

You must collect contact information from your guests in order to communicate with them electronically. The way in which you collect your customers' contact information will make all the difference in their willingness to give it. One method is via an intake form. Your guests will be familiar with this process because they do it at other businesses. On the form you will collect first and last name, telephone number, and email address. Some clients might be skeptical about giving this information, so I also suggest that on the form you tell them what you plan to do with their data. Remember, explaining what you're doing and setting expectations upfront is always a good idea and when collecting information it is no different. It could read something like this:

> "This salon provides (will one day provide) online communication for your convenience. You may choose to receive your confirmations via email or text message, request appointments online, refer your friends via email, submit satisfaction surveys and receive special offers. We will never share or sell your information to any other party."

If you choose to do electronic communication, your front desk staff needs to make data collection a routine part of operations as quickly as possible, and they must understand that getting this information is critical to the long-term success of the salon.

When to Communicate

To Confirm Appointments

Consider giving your guests the option to confirm visits with you via email or text message. They often prefer the less intrusive form of an email or text more than a phone call. Electronic communications will reduce the time that your front desk staff spends on the phone, allowing your staff to focus more on educating and selling retail products to guests, pre-booking follow-up appointments, and ensuring guest satisfaction. Spending less time making confirmation calls can help you turn the front desk cost center into a guest services profit center.

To Retain Customers

Retention of new and existing clients is one of the biggest indicators of the success of your salon. Focusing on repeat business from guests should be high on your priority list when it comes to contacting your customers. Here are three key communication strategies that can help you retain your guests.

1. Say Thank You

Your main goal with this communication is to make sure that your guests feel comfortable and welcomed back. Thank you communications should be sent within 24-48 hours after your guest has been in the salon. Your guest should feel appreciated for choosing your salon over any other. You can do this automatically via email and software programs designed for this function, or you can go the old-fashioned route of a handwritten note, which can be a nice touch for first-time guests. Your thank you letter should include appreciation for their last visit, information on their next appointment or how to schedule another appointment, other services offered in the salon that they might want to take advantage of, and details about your referral program. The most important element of a thank you message is a survey. Especially as you get started, it is important to ask guests how you can improve.

2. Surveys

Surveying your repeat and new guests should be a part of your retention strategy, whether you've been open two months or twenty years. By asking key questions, you can help ensure quality of service and you can use the feedback as a coaching tool for your team.

Example survey questions:

- Were you greeted in a prompt and friendly manner?
- Were all services performed to your satisfaction?
- How would you rate your service provider?
- How would you rate overall cleanliness?
- Do you prefer online confirmations to phone calls?
- Would you return? (Helps measure retention)
- Would you refer a friend? (Helps attract new guests)

3. Beauty Reminders

Pre-booking should always be one of your top goals in the salon, but no matter what you offer or how hard you try, you'll never reach 100%. You will always have guests who will opt not to pre-book, and for those clients I suggest beauty reminders. This is a gentle reminder via email, text, postcard or phone call that they have not been to see you in a while. It gives them an easy way to request their next appointment. Sending these types of reminders helps the client and can help you increase your frequency of visits if timed properly.

CHAPTER 16

Marketing Your Salon Online

"Social networking helps reach people easier and quicker."
— Bill Cosby

The first task concerning marketing your salon online is making an educated decision whether you want an online presence and what kind of presence you want. The Internet provides tremendous opportunity to reach a lot of people fairly easily. You can keep in touch with your current customers and reach new customers. In fact, many people looking for services today only search online, and you will miss an opportunity with these customers if you do not have a web presence.

The flip side is that, with social media, you cannot control everything that is said about you online. The CEO of Amazon once said, "If you make customers unhappy in the physical world, they might each tell 6 friends. If you make customers unhappy on the Internet, they can each tell 6,000 friends." Of course, an unhappy customer can blast you on the Internet whether you have a Facebook page or not. But the more presence you have on the web, the more time you will have to spend monitoring, and possibly responding to, what is said about you.

Even so, in today's world it is probably best to take advantage of online marketing opportunities. This is especially true if you are building a new business or trying to expand your business or if you have a younger clientele. Assuming you do embrace the opportunity the web offers, this chapter will give you some pointers on effectively managing your web presence.

Search Engines

Google is the number one search engine in the world. It is important that you manage your listing on Google Places as this is often the first impression that a potential guest has of your business. To do this, simply go to http://www.google.com/places/ and claim your listing, by clicking on "Business Owner" at the top right of the page and following the instructions. Once you have followed the steps you will be able to add photos (your logo for brand awareness and a picture of the outside of your salon to help clients with navigation from mobile devices), list your specialties, and comment back to any reviews that are written about you.

People are going to write reviews about your business, but it's up to you to manage your reputation. You can do this by responding to those reviews online. If the review is positive, thank them for it. If the review is negative, apologize and offer to make it up to them. This will show the online world that you are a conscientious business owner.

Other sites to consider checking on and claiming are Citysearch.com, Bing.com/local, yp.com, dexknows.com, local.yahoo.com, and yelp.com.

Facebook

Social media marketing can be very important to the future of a business. Facebook is the second most visited website in the United States. The salon industry has a unique opportunity to thrive via social media because of the closeness of the guest with her salon and her consumption of beauty-related retail items. Each of your clients who connects with you on Facebook is also connected to an average of 150 other people who are likely to be in the same region and similar demographic. Use "viral marketing" to its fullest advantage. Viral marketing is using an existing social network (Facebook) to help promote your brand. In your case, you want your customers to "like," "share" or "comment" on posts that you make on Facebook, because doing so will create buzz within their social network about you!

Here are a few steps:

1. Encourage each of your guests to check into Facebook when they arrive at the salon. You can encourage this by doing token giveaways like complimentary samples if they check in. Checking-in alerts their friends to the businesses and sites they visit, which gets your name brand out to more people similar to your client.

2. Ask your guests to "like" you on Facebook. Give them a good reason, such as periodic specials or last minute deals.

3. Try to post to your wall once a day. Consider which types of articles or posts your clients would be most likely to comment on or share with their friends.

Four types of successful Facebook posts:

1. Those that show your personality: Try pictures of the team, before and after pictures, any community events you participate in, wedding/baby announcements, and so forth.

2. Those that educate or inform: Share an article about how to manage dry hair in the winter, Fashion Week pictures, product information, or product sales.

3. Those that engage: Ask a question or encourage comments. Ask for an opinion on a new hair color or style, or which new nail color they like best.

4. Those that just ask for what you want: "Like, Share or Comment on this picture (of XYZ product) by 2:00 pm to be entered in a drawing to win a full-size bottle!" I've seen easily 40-50 likes in a several-hour window from posts like these. They really have a tendency to go viral.

While it's important to have as many followers as you can, the more important metric is to know how many people are talking about you on Facebook. The more people are talking about you, the more likely they are to click onto your page. Once you get them on your page you will want to give them an action item; for example, to request an appointment by giving them a phone number to call or a web form to fill out. All this Facebooking is for nothing if you aren't getting people in the chair!

To invest in the future of your salon, you must invest in communicating to your customers. If you want to become the beauty expert for your clients, connect with them in the way that is most convenient and meaningful for them, provide great service, and listen to their feedback. They will make you a regular part of their lives for many years to come.

Communication with Customers Outside the Salon

★ Your brand says who you are, make sure it projects the image you want.

★ Keep up communications with your customers even when they're not in for a visit, using follow-on correspondence to thank customers, confirm appointments, and send reminders.

★ Contact your customers in the way that works best for them and you, probably electronically.

★ Let social media work for you with an effective online presence.

★ Make sure when customers Google salons they find you and reach out to them daily through Facebook postings.

Customer Retention

CHAPTER 17

VIP Service Only Starts with Their Name

"Everyone has an invisible sign hanging from their neck saying, 'Make me feel important.' Never forget this message when working with people."

— Mary Kay Ash

Why are we focused on making sure we have a beautiful salon, wonderful rapport with our customers, and an awesome brand? Is it to keep our customers satisfied, to keep them happy, to keep them looking great? It's to keep them ... period!

Retain customers. They are the most important part of any business. Your customers are your lifeline to profits, respect and reputation. No business can survive without customer retention, but it can be hard work to retain customers and keep them coming back for more of your services or product offerings. However, it is even harder work to continually gain new customers, so going the extra mile to retain your current customer base will positively impact your profits and business status in the community.

Customer retention begins with building relationships, not just client lists. And great customer relationships start with VIP service. VIP service, in turn, starts with their name.

Knowing your client's name, and using it at every opportunity, tells your client that you know who they are. You see them. As their stylist, you touch them more than once in any given service. Touching is personal—you should know their name. Have you encountered an acquaintance and cannot recall their name? That makes them feel very unimportant! You don't want your customers to feel like a VUPs (very unimportant persons) instead of a VIPs when they have a service done in your salon.

In business it can be extremely hard to learn and remember each client or guest's name, but with today's technology the only thing you need to do is look up your next appointment's name on the salon's software. Not so hard considering their personal information is at your fingertips. If this is too difficult for you, then have the front desk person text their name to your phone. (Don't generally like phones at the service station, but at least you're making an attempt to provide VIP all the way.)

The intimate environment of the salon provides a unique opportunity to apply and repeat VIP treatment. Use this intimacy to build and engage in good relationships with your customers. The closeness will enable a bond that most business owners and their staff cannot accomplish and wish they had.

You can use technology to help you. Your point of sale or other software can capture all details of the VIP: birthday, anniversary, holidays. You can use this information to personalize your marketing, for example sending a greeting or voucher on their birthday or first service anniversary. You can also use technology (or index cards, if you're a techo-phobe), to remember other more personal information - kids, an upcoming special event they talked about, etc. - things that you can ask them about on their next visit. Of course, you're also capturing their preferences about your services and products. The more information you have on each client, the closer relationship you can have with them and the more you can understand and meet their needs.

Above all, the VIP is exactly that. All customers are important and special and should be treated with 5-star service. Your salon's business survival is based on each customer who walks through your salon's front door. By letting them know they are VIPs to you, these customers will rise from casual patronage, to enthusiastic, loyal supporters.

CHAPTER 18

Keeping Clients for Life

*"Revolve your world around the customer and more
customers will revolve around you."*

— Heather Williams

The goal of any business is to attract and keep customers. You can work in the most luxurious salon, spa, or men's grooming salon but if your customer service and attitude are not up to par, that will determine whether your customers keep coming back. All businesses want their customers to come back. When they do come, we want them to stay. So why is it that no matter what you do they sometimes don't come back? There are many reasons, and some you just can't control.

Why they don't come back is a tough question and the answers are not always about you or the salon you work in. Sometimes people just move on. There is no particular reason—maybe they just don't have the need for that service anymore; maybe they moved away. There are, however, other clients who do not return because of you, your salon and the services you offer.

Things You Can't Control

Below are some factors that you cannot control—no matter what you do, they will occur through the course of your career.

Customers move - Approximately 5 percent of your customers will move away. They will move for many reasons, none of which you can control.

Customers' relatives or friends become competitors - You may be the best hairstylist, barber, massage therapist or esthetician but people meet other people. Let's say you have a great client, but her brother marries a woman who is a hairstylist. Guess what, your customer will try her sister-in-law. She is obligated to and if she is any good, there goes your customer. You can't control this and this is absolutely no fault of your own. There is an old expression "blood is thicker than water." If you plan on having a long career in hair this will definitely happen to you at some point.

Customers die - One percent of your customers will die. We're all going to die at some point. There is not much you can do about one of your clients passing on. Through the course of your career this happens. No matter what industry you're in, you will lose clients, coworkers, family or friends. It is part of life. Although it is not a big part of customer loss, it will happen and will be tough for you to deal with and get through.

Controlling the Things You Can

One must always think about how to keep their clients happy in the service business. If you stop worrying about client satisfaction or caring whether your client is happy or unhappy with the service you provide, then at that point you should think about changing your career.

To keep customers, you should focus on the issues you can control. There are many ways to improve your service level if you slow down and listen to your client and others. Remember your client has many other salons, barbershops or spas to visit—probably within 100 yards from your present location. Competition is tough. There are ten service values that you should always follow that will help you keep your clients for life.

1. Build strong relationships with clients.

2. Always be responsive to the expressed and unexpressed wishes and needs of your client.

3. Be empowered to create unique, memorable, and personal experiences for your client.

4. Understand your role in your place of business.

5. Own and immediately resolve client problems.

6. Create a work environment of teamwork.

7. Treat your coworker's client as if your own.

8. Continuously look at ways to learn and grow.

9. Always protect the privacy of your clients. Loose lips sink ships and cause clients to go elsewhere.

10. Always be proud of your profession, appearance, language, and behavior.

Staying on top of the things you can control will help you retain your customers. There are some issues that fall into both the controllable and the uncontrollable categories. In these cases, you obviously focus on what you can do.

Customers don't like your products - Approximately 15 percent of your customers will leave because they are dissatisfied with the products your salon sells. If the majority of your customers do like your products, this may be a case of you can't please everybody. The reality is some products are a better fit for some customers and work better for them on their hair or skin. However, if most of your customers don't like your products (they either tell you or aren't buying), it's probably time to switch product lines.

Poor Attitude - The biggest reason clients don't come back is because of attitude. The worst part about this is that it may not be your attitude. When a guest steps into the salon, barbershop, spa or medical spa many things can go wrong.

- Your client bumps into a nasty client leaving the salon and they have words.

- The front desk person doesn't give your client the time of day.

- Your client sits and waits for you and no one gives them an update or lets them know you're running late.

- A coworker says something to your client that is inappropriate.

Unfortunately, this happens in the service business. Some of your customers will not come back because they feel they were not treated right and they perceived an attitude of indifference from you or a coworker. It is true that indifference is a natural enemy of any service-driven business. No matter how hard you try, there will be a time in your career that a customer to whom you have given the best hairstyle and color just does not come back. You can ponder forever and try to guess what went wrong, but it all comes down to indifference. That person just didn't like something you or someone in your organization said or a way they acted.

You can't always control what others do, and you can't control how someone will react to what others do. You can teach and encourage your staff to all be VIP providers following the guidelines provided in this book, which will decrease the chance they do something that upsets a client. You can also follow the advice for handling conflict to try to diffuse situations.

Bad Service - I have been told many times that the difference between a good haircut and a bad haircut is two weeks. Well, that's how long it takes a bad haircut to grow out and not look that bad anymore! I hope you never have to use that explanation when a client complains about a cut or style you just gave them.

Your customer may feel they received a bad haircut or color or facial. If this is the case, no matter what you do, that customer will probably never come back. Unless they are very loyal or are a close friend or relative, they are most likely gone forever. Your service levels always have to be top-notch. It has to be game on every day you step into your place of business. A poor haircut or color job is inexcusable. If you have a service provider giving poor service, you have to let this person go. Not only will a poorly serviced client not come back, they are a walking bad advertisement for your salon.

Move on when things you can't control impact your customer base, and continue providing VIP service to keep and attract other clients. But also stay on top of those things you can control in order to keep the majority of your customers happy and coming back.

CHAPTER 19

The VVIP Customers

"Do what you do so well that they will want to see it again and bring their friends."

– Walt Disney

Y ou opened your salon with the thought of being the best salon in your area. You have implemented procedures with your staff that have your salon team understanding that customer satisfaction is the top priority in your salon. Everyone on your team is on board and everything seems perfect, but you want to step it up a notch and raise the bar on your customer satisfaction. You now want to offer your clients the best service standards possible—VIP service is your goal.

Customers are customers, and each one is as important as the next. Which customers do you plan on offering your VIP service to? Think about this for a minute. Have you decided? The answer is simple; every one of your customers deserves your new upgraded VIP service. Treat each of your customers as VIPs no matter how hard it is to dissociate their differences. Remember, no matter how difficult it is to offer VIP service to each of your customers, your rewards will be endless when it comes to customer satisfaction and business growth.

Still, every business has its best customers, so how do you recognize and reward these important clients? It isn't necessarily a factor of how much they spend, although the biggest spender on the planet would certainly qualify. But it could also be a long-standing client who's been loyal over the years, or the client who has referred so many friends and acquaintances they're like a client recruiter.

For these VVIPs (Very Very Important Persons), firstname Holmes, title, (tell who Holmes is here…) says you've got to give them the personal touch. Any reward you give them has to be thoughtful. One way to do this is to give them an experience, something you know they'll never forget and which they will always associate with you. "It could be a day at the races or a voucher for a spa day," advises Holmes. "If it is specifically aimed at them, it shows you are thinking about them."

Another possibility is to give them a free service they haven't tried before. Maybe you've been cutting a VVIP customer's hair for years, but she's never tried color. Offer to do it free for her birthday. Not only will you get brownie points for remembering her special day and just plain being nice, there's also a potential big upside. The cost of the free color is mostly your time, but the potential benefit if she decides to continue coloring in the future could make you the real winner here.

Make Them Part of Your Business

It is crucial to make your special clients feel a part of your business. Sometimes, it means you have to think out of the box. If your distributor is offering education to your staff, include some of your clients. Have them come in for a free service and use them as models. Involving them will bring them closer to you and your staff.

If you are having a "Ladies Night Out," include some clients to make them feel special. They may not participate, but the invitation will surely let them know that they were considered. Sometimes, the thought is all that matters in making someone's day.

Build Partnerships

Holmes also points to the special service she enjoys at one of her favorite local boutiques, where she's often offered a glass of bubbly or a coffee. It's one of those special small businesses that regularly goes above and beyond what customers expect, which means they come back time and time again. "They once sourced a top for me to go with an outfit I had bought from them," she says.

The boutique also collaborates with the dry cleaners across the road and they will alter things quickly at no cost to the customer. Partnerships like this are a great way to save customers time and money and they can be a win-win for all parties.

Go the Extra Mile

What does it mean to go the extra mile? Holmes provides the example of a cab firm that she used for years and recommended to all her friends. The firm did so well it was eventually sold based on its extensive clientele.

What did this cab firm do that was so special? "It was like being picked up by a friend," says Holmes. "There were a core team of excellent drivers who my neighbors and colleagues got to know quickly. The first time they picked me up to go to the airport, Peter ran around the garden to help me capture the cat. And Kenny used to pick me up from the station and we'd go to M&S on the way home."

You may still be wondering if it is okay to differentiate between one client and another. The answer is yes, if you want to reward a particularly important customer, but not if it means offering two standards of service. "You should never differentiate overtly," says Holmes. "Covertly you can offer special services to top customers. But you should never show different levels of respect and courtesy. You must treat everyone as special."

Treating customers like VIPs is not rocket science. You need to start with a "do as I would be done by" approach and build up from there. To be really successful, you need to build relationships. Think about how you can go the extra mile for your extra-special customers. Then aim for both surprise and delight by exceeding their expectations.

CHAPTER 20

VIP Service for Males in the Salon

"Your customer doesn't care how much you know until they know how much you care."
—Damon Richards

M and hair—sounds like this should be an easy task to accomplish. There are plenty of men in the world and most have plenty of hair. No brainer, right? Giving men some VIP service for services as simple as a haircut and maybe a shave should be almost impossible to screw up, right? Well, yes and certainly no. Basically it all comes down to some very important facts. Understanding these facts is key to giving men exactly what they want and need, and awarding them with the service they deserve in your salon.

First Things First . . . Education

When offering services to men in an upscale salon environment we should make sure we're prepared to deliver. So often I get booked to teach classes on men's services in either a very elite hair school or a very high-end or upscale salon and spa. This tells me that either they don't receive much training in men's cutting in school or they're not receiving training focused on exclusive men's cutting. So in order to offer the best we can to male clients, we need to make sure that we regularly conduct training and education that is focused on men's cutting and styling. Not all men's hair is easy to cut and yes, they do ask for different cuts and styles. This all goes back to the cosmetology school you graduated from.

Many times young cosmetologists are able to latch on to a mentor in the salon they work in to learn everything this person is willing to share. In life I find that these people can teach you more in a matter of a few short months than any school in the country. Stay close and listen. You will be surprised how much you will pick up from them and be able to include in your focus on giving VIP service to your male clients.

Making the Salon Male Friendly

We should start by making the salon or spa male friendly. Let's make sure that we have things like male friendly magazines (GQ, Details, Esquire, Men's Health, and so forth) in the waiting area. If wine and cocktails are offered, add some beers for the guys. When conducting hair color on males, keep a supply of inexpensive black T-shirts in variety of sizes for the guys as opposed to smocks—they'll feel more masculine in them. Offer hot towel/barbershop facials at shampoo bowls or hot towel head/neck massages following a haircut. Do neck clean ups with a nape razor (legal for cosmetologists as well) with some shaving lather or conditioner if permitted. Turn on "male" conversation when conversing with an average guy: "Catch the playoffs?" or "How's business?" Simple as that, right?

> *Example* - Here's how to converse in "guy talk" when you find yourself in a conversation you may not know anything about. Every morning when you're having your morning cup of Joe, tea, or Mojo juice that gets you going, pick up your local paper. You don't have to read the whole thing, but quickly go through the paper and yes, more importantly, the local business and sports section. This will prepare you for any topics that may come up. You will not be an expert but you will surely be able to carry on a conversation. This will quickly move you up as an "in the know" hairstylist. VIP at its best!

What keeps the men coming back?

Offer incentives for services for very regular male clients. Here are two down and dirty quickies one expert uses for regulars: a complimentary haircut after every 12th service, or half-off an executive manicure/massage with a haircut (note that offering a service they haven't used before may get them to try something new and make a believer of them!)

Educate male clients on grooming products such as proper shampoos, conditioners, and styling products—whatever best fits their needs. If they don't buy it from you they'll get it somewhere else, right? Bottom line is we have to welcome, service, and invite our male clients back in a way that makes them feel they are welcome in the salon, and that the salon has elements that are geared especially toward them and make them feel special. Now let's get that salon male friendly!

PART V - SUMMARY

Customer Retention

★ Retaining customers is your top priority.

★ Make sure you get to know your customers and take advantage of the intimate environment of the salon to build close relationships.

★ Don't worry about things you can't control, but focus on the things you can control to keep customers coming back.

★ It is appropriate to sometimes give your extra special customers some extra special attention.

★ Make sure your salon environment and services welcome all customers, including men.

PART VI

Quality Products Complement Quality Service

CHAPTER 21

Selecting the Right Products for Your Salon

"A lot of times people don't know what they want until you show it to them."

— Steve Jobs

Choosing products for your shop to display and sell will be an important decision to make. Selling retail is another business in and of itself that is housed within your salon or spa. The choices you make about which products to sell is extremely important. The options are limitless and the task may be overwhelming. Not only should there be a demand for your products, but it must be profitable and something you and your staff enjoy selling. Before you commit to a product line, consider the following factors:

Marketability

In today's retail world, finding and picking the right products to sell to your clients is the key to success. You and your clients see so many brands on television, in magazines, and on the Internet. What works better or is more marketable?

If you the pick wrong products, your clients won't buy them. If products are priced too high or aren't meeting current trends, you could be stuck with a ton of inventory and very little sales. Before considering what products to sell, determine your market and your clientele. Once you know what kind of client and the desired market to target, choosing the right brands will be much easier.

Next, investigate the products that sell in your area. Inspect and visit other salons as a client. However, do not fall for the pretense that if every salon in the area has a product, it must be good—that is not always the case. It's good to be different. If you don't like the look, smell, and feel of the products you are thinking about providing, it will be difficult for you to market and sell them to your clients. It's essential that the brands you choose to carry match with your target—your market clientele. Some of your clients will buy high-priced products; others may buy only low- or mid-priced products. The key is to provide a selection that is appealing to your larger client population.

Education and Training

Choosing a long-standing manufacturer that supports your salon with marketing materials, education, and training will position you and your staff for increased sales. Education is the key! You must know all the features and benefits of the entire product line and learn the best ways to showcase the products to your clients. Manufacturers may offer educational events right in your salon on new products; and they may promote your salon on their website. They have trained consultants and business partners to assist with education from the front of your salon to the back. These consultants and partners can help guide you with business decisions. These are all key items that you may not have been aware of when deciding on a product line to carry. Don't think small business, think big. Aligning yourself and your salon with a big name can make or break your retail business.

Profit Margin

Selling expensive products is usually more profitable, but requires more investment in inventory costs and more credibility. When you are picking your retail goods, there is a lot you have to keep in mind in order to run a profit. You'll need to consider the direct and indirect costs that have to be added to the price of each item you sell. You must remember all the overhead expenses you have in the salon before establishing a price point. Also, don't forget about commissions to your employees. The best-selling products in your salon will never earn a profit if your margins are too small. Your manufacturer's representative should be able to assist you with pricing in order for you to maintain the correct profits.

Consumable Items

The best thing about selling salon products is the recurring sales. Many salons carry other items such styling tools. Those items take up expensive space in your retail area. A consumable item that needs to be replaced on a regular basis, such as shampoos, sprays, and conditioners is a great way to create long-term sales. By establishing a clientele with recurring product sales, clients will become more loyal and continue to come back to you again and again for all their salon services and products. When your client picks up that bottle of shampoo at home and it's empty, she will immediately think of where she bought it. That bottle of shampoo is a daily reminder of you and your salon.

What's Hot and What's Not

When it comes to selecting your brands, you need to see what's hot in the industry. Beauty trade magazines and industry trade shows will give you a good indication of what's hot and what's not. Certain magazines, such as Allure, Cosmo, and Elle, will help indicate what is hot. Have a staff meeting on current trends. You may also have some students joining your team. They should know the new products that have been introduced in their school and have a better idea of what products are currently popular.

Competition

It is good and healthy to have competition and you can outsell them in retail if you market and display your products well. The location of your products is very important. Hiding products under a counter, behind your reception desk, or locked in a cabinet will not help you sell product. You might as well put a sign over the items saying "do not touch."

Products must be on display as soon as you walk in your salon. The client must feel at home in your retail area. Make buying your products fun and have items that everyone can afford. Handsome display cases, easy access, and an educated staff will ensure that you sell more products than your competition. Have your staff talk about the products they use. You want your clients to go home with something. Manufacturers have small sample bottles or teaser items. Having products like this, in sample sizes, will allow your clients to try out your products and will entice them to come back and buy the next time.

Diversity

Keep your product offerings simple in the early stages of your opening. If your product line is narrow and focused, then your marketing efforts can be just as tightly focused, which will bring you the best results for your marketing dollars. As your business grows, so can your product line, as long as you keep new products compatible with your market and according to clients' needs and the local demands.

The most important thing you should ask yourself is, "Would I give this product to my best friend or use it myself?"

CHAPTER 22

The Importance of Vendor Relationships

"Businesses must invest in products and people in order to create new wealth."

— John Hoeven

Have you ever heard it's not what you know, it's who you know that can make or break you? My father once told me to go out in the world and make friends with as many people as I could. I asked him how is that possible, and why? He grabbed me by the shoulders, sat me down, looked me in the eyes and said, "Son, the more people you know in life the easier it will be for you, your family, and your career, and I promise that if you do this, many good things will come of it."

That life lesson was many years ago, and the lesson I learned is that in life it's not what you know (yes, that helps), but it's who you know that will help you get the right job, help you with business decisions, find you an attorney, get you a good doctor when needed, get the plumbing fixed when it is broken … the list is endless. You need to understand that in business you need to get to know the right people. Why, you might ask, and who?

Start with the people who can directly help you and your business every day—your distributor sales representative and manufacturer sales person. Let's take a quick look at how they can help your salon business. They can get you much needed product for your salon, education for your staff, tickets to beauty shows, a new hot stylist from another salon and deeper discounts on your retail and back bar. The list is endless, and I can go on for hours about this topic but what I want to drive home is that getting to know the right people will help you and your business when you need it the most.

By developing an appropriate bond with your vendors, you'll benefit from far more than just promptly returned calls or hassle-free service; you'll also tap into their insider's network of sales tips and tactics.

Remember, they've been dealing with many salons and have seen more plans succeed and fail than you can imagine, and you can benefit from their experience. If you have the right relationship, that is.

Why You Need a Strong Vendor Relationship

Your primary relationship as a retail salon is with your clients. They're bringing in the money, the bodies, the recommendations and the sales, so you should do whatever you can (within reason) to keep that relationship alive and well. The second most important business relationship you have may well be with your vendors.

A strong vendor relationship has many potential benefits for your salon and can end up being an asset to your business. Have you thought about product returns, new product lines, payment terms, delivery? So have they.

How a Strong Vendor Relationship can Help

- **Product Returns** – Many times, suppliers will have restocking fees for returned merchandise. If you and your vendor are on good terms (and you've been diligent about paying in full, on time, every time), they may be able to waive restocking fees, shipping or other charges/penalties associated with returning unused or unsold products.

- **New Product Lines** – Imagine being the first salon on the block to have a new product or tool. With a good working relationship, you can be the first person your vendor thinks of when approaching clients about exclusive or semi-exclusive products. At the very least, they may give you extra samples or test products to use and demonstrate at no cost.

- **Payment Terms** – As long as you've been maintaining your account and it's in good standing, your vendor may be able to work with you on payment terms for products your salon needs. They may be able to extend a line of credit to you rather than ask for payment up front, which would allow you to put product on the shelves and in the hands of clients, which puts money in the bank, and which lets you pay the vendor in full.

- **Product Delivery** – Having trouble expediting an order? A quick call to your vendor can help. Your vendor can also help with shipping costs and put in a rush order when your supply hits critical low points.

Building Your Vendor Relationship

Building your vendor relationship is not unlike building any friendship —find the common ground and take it from there. You and your vendor have built-in common ground—the product. The rest can grow from that. Find out about their interests, their personal life, their past. In that information, you'll find common ground and places to bond.

It's important to remember to listen more than you talk; that gives you the information you may need later to make an informed decision on how to proceed with your vendor. By this, we mean that you should take your cues from the vendor. If they're funny and joking, be funny and joking back; if they're all business, keep the small talk small and get to it; if they're open to talking about their family, life or history, be open to sharing yours.

Some things to keep in mind when communicating with vendors:

- Vendors are people too; treat them with respect and kindness and they'll treat you the same.

- Vendors are busy. Like you, vendors have multiple clients and aren't always able to drop what they're doing and switch tasks. How do you feel when demanding clients come in the salon? Don't make your vendors feel the same way.

- A little patience, understanding, and empathy go a long way. Give vendors time to answer emails and return phone calls.

- Be honest with vendors about product orders, pricing and payment options because they may have creative options at their disposal. If you're having trouble meeting a minimum, they may have another client in the same situation and you may be able to split an order to reach minimums.

- Be open to conversation. No, you don't need to spend 30 minutes chatting it up with a vendor, but a little personal talk can go a long way to solidify a relationship.

It comes down to this piece of advice: treat others as you would like to be treated. Remember, you don't have to be best friends with your vendor, but you do have to be friendly with them.

Quality Products Complement Quality Service

★ Your product offerings need to fit your clientele and your brand image.

★ Your staff should be educated on the features and benefits of the product line.

★ Use what you sell and let customers know which products you're using.

★ Build strong relationships with your distributor and manufacturer sales people.

★ Vendors can benefit your business by working with you on new product lines, returns, payment terms and expediting deliveries.

A 5-Star Staff

CHAPTER 23

Quality Service Providers for Your Salon

"Start with good people, lay out the rules, communicate with your employees, motivate them and reward them. If you do all these things effectively, you can't miss."

—Lee Iacocca

Having the right team working in your salon or spa is critical to the success of the salon. Your service providers must be well-trained and exceptional at what they do. Each client that leaves the salon is like a live billboard, walking around showing the cut, color and style they got at your salon; needless to say, the end results must be consistently beautiful. In addition to having great skills, your providers must also have great attitudes. Their commitment and dedication to providing 5-star service should match your own. A salon owner's job is to hire, train and keep a great staff.

Hiring

The first step in hiring quality service providers for your salon is building a relationship with cosmetology schools who maintain high standards and graduation rates. It is important to build a rapport with area cosmetology establishments in order to stay informed about current events involving both students and staff, such as career and demonstration days. These events allow students and staff of the cosmetology establishment to become familiar with your salon, while also allowing management to see the personalities of students in their learning environment. It is vital to become involved in advisory boards at cosmetology schools, which provide opportunities for salon owners to give feedback to the cosmetology establishment regarding what they would like to see in new hires.

Selectively choosing service providers ensures a standard of quality performance; thereby building on the reputation and success of your salon. When preparing yourself to hire service providers, find out if the cosmetology schools you have a relationship with have a placement program. If the students in surrounding establishments do not seem like a good fit for your salon, be prepared to travel to another city in search of a future employee. The retention rate of service providers at your salon can increase by as much as 80 percent if you are willing to invest the time and energy into the hiring process.

During the interview process, it is important to review the applicant's high school and cosmetology school attendance records. Their attendance at school is a possible indication of the employee's future attendance habits at your salon. It is often beneficial to ask the interviewee to describe someone who has been a role model in their life. Their answer will give you possible insight to the character and work ethic of this potential employee. In order to finalize which student is the best fit for your salon, have the student perform a full makeover or work alongside you for a day.

Trial Period

Upon hiring, make it clear that you are hiring him or her on a trial or temporary basis, easing the dismissal of an employee who is not meeting expectations. It is essential that all team members are made aware of current expectations and job descriptions. Meeting with new employees daily instills teamwork and the salon's values and ethics with the employee. Setting aside 15 minutes each day during their trial period to meet with the team member provides an opportunity to discuss daily goals, enabling the employee to take ownership for his or her daily performance. Implementing a training program to test and guide employees is a fundamental growth-building tool which can assist in long-term employee performance.

Train, Track and Reward

A new employee has to be taught your way of doing business. You should let them know your expectations on appearance and client communication, including how to consult with the client about their service as well as how to establish and maintain a good personal rapport with the client, and how to sell products or other services. Make sure you give clear explanations of what is important and what is expected when working with clients in your salon. This book may be used as a basis for educating a new provider on how to give quality service.

Once you have taught employees your expectations, you want to verify they are implementing the things they've learned. Rate them on their appearance, check the language they choose when talking with the client, and listen to the topics that they talk about. Make sure they have the correct knowledge on the products and services you offer. Every now and then, test your employees. But, don't set them up for failure. Let them know that you will be doing "pop quizzes on Tuesdays" to test everyone's knowledge about a new product line or about the new customer service guidelines that you reviewed at the last staff meeting.

When you catch people in the act of doing exactly as you want and expect, give them an "on-the-spot" reward. It can be as simple as saying, "Mary, I really like how you reviewed all the features and benefits of the new frizz control product line with your client. I think you should jot down what you said so that we can share the script with the other team members. Looks like it worked too. I saw that she bought the shampoo and conditioner before she left today. Great job!" You can also have gift cards to places like local movie theatres, Starbucks, gas cards, etc. Use these as rewards when your employees meet their daily, weekly, or monthly goals.

We also believe that the employee attitude will determine their "altitude" in their career and their financial success. Look for their demeanor, posture, personality, and confidence. A grading system will help the new employee have clear and concise knowledge of your salon's expectations.

The results will determine the quality of service that this employee will give your clients, and the relationships that they will build for your salon. With this measurement system in place, you will see the new employee give your client a "wow" factor, meaning the client got more in service than they expected. Doing so will ensure that you have a 5-star salon and team.

Empower

One warning: be careful not to micromanage your team, especially as they gain more experience. This may stunt creativity. Employees with an open mind will be more receptive to learning. Employees who engage in effective communication with both clients and team members often create an unforgettable customer service experience. Your goal is to eventually have employees who are so good at their job, they don't need you to tell them what to do; they just need you to enable them to do it by providing a great facility and working environment.

By empowering your staff, they may surprise you with some of the things they come up with, and unexpected services sometimes bring the most value. They may have suggestions that will help all of your team. A wise man once told me he would walk in the back door of his businesses and talk to everyone on the way up to the front. By the time he made it to the front, he had a good "pulse" on what was happening in his businesses. As your staff will look to you for direction, consider posting a positive thought daily to inspire your team. Always set a positive example, know what's going on in your salon and be generous with kudos when a provider does a great job.

The salon business is a finicky business. Keeping your staff on board and from jumping ship always has to be a concern. Being a salon that constantly offers 5-star service, décor and extra touches, makes it extremely hard for any of your employees to duplicate what you are offering on their own or with someone else. By empowering your team and letting them know you appreciate them, they are also more likely to stick around.

CHAPTER 24

A Great Gatekeeper

"Be everywhere, do everything, and never fail to astonish the customer."

—Macy's Motto

Horizontal how many times have we walked into a place of business and we were not greeted by someone? It may be a clothing store, restaurant, doctor's office, or a beauty salon. How does that make you feel?

We find ourselves wondering if we should leave. Is the place open for business? We don't know if we should sit or stand or yell hello to see if someone is going to help. The importance of a gatekeeper is crucial to your business.

Historically, the gatekeeper has had many job titles, such as receptionist, secretary, or salesperson. What matters most is not the title, but that you realize how critical this person is to the success of your business.

This is the first person your clients meet when they walk into your salon. He or she is the first person who speaks on behalf of your company when a potential client calls or an existing one makes an appointment, or a distributor calls for assistance in placing a product order. In essence, this person speaks for you and is an extension of you and your salon's brand.

Hiring

When hiring, have you thought about the personality and character of this individual? Are you certain this person is outgoing and enjoys being around people? There are certain things you should look for when hiring this person. Listed below are several key items to keep in mind when you are interviewing for your gatekeeper:

- Basic understanding of the beauty industry and terminology
- Appearance is very important
- Should have basic research skills
- Outgoing, "people person"
- Should understand and be able to use all office equipment
- Handle all phone calls
- Desire to take charge
- Understanding and ability to use salon's software
- Sales background
- Willing to work full-time, including weekends
- Capable of being your right-hand person
- Capable of handling money
- Trustworthy
- Willing to manage

When hiring your gatekeeper, be sure to ask:
- What type of computer skills do you have?
- Have you ever deposited money at a bank?
- Have you done credit card processing before?
- Are you able and capable of opening and closing the salon?
- Can you work weekends?
- What type of phone skills do you have?
- Do you understand and follow time management?
- Can you take a tough phone call?
- How do you handle people who are rude or upset?
- What kind of sales experience do you have?

High turnover is often caused by not having the "right person for the right position." Often, salon owners or managers are hiring out of emergency due to an immediate opening at the front desk. To find the right person, get focused, get organized, and get prepared for the recruiting and interview process. First, you should plan on finding and interviewing several candidates, not just one or two.

The best way to recruit for this position is to find someone that already has customer service and sales experience and possesses "sales charisma." Keep your eyes and ears open for your next front desk person through your own customer service experiences. When it's time to interview, tailor the interview questions around the important duties of a front desk sales support staff. Remember, the front desk is the first impression, the last impression, and often the lasting impression of the salon.

If you put an ad in the paper, on craigslist.com, or other places, be sure to put your ad in the Sales section, not the Receptionist section. This is a sales position.

During the interview, make sure to explain all the sales responsibilities the front desk team has, including offering additional services, pre-booking the next appointment, closing the retail sale, taking clients on a salon tour, offering sales and promotions, etc.

One interview technique involves handing your pen to the person you are interviewing. Using this performance-based interviewing technique will allow you to see how well they can describe the features and benefits of the pen and offer the sale of the pen to you. Plus, you'll be able to test and see how brave their sales skills really are! You will find, or eliminate, many candidates with this simple exercise. Try it!

Training

The key to running a successful front desk is continuous training on your retail products, software updates, expected marketing, and the owner's beliefs and expected business tactics. Without training you can't expect this person to run and manage a successful front desk operation. Below are some of the key guidelines to running a salon front desk.

- Always be clean and organized.
- Make sure staff looks professional.
- Always have a smile.

- Always greet the customer by their first name and give them a big hello, nice to see you.

- Make sure to ask clients how their service and experience was.

- Make sure you ask which products they like would like to purchase. If they are purchasing products, ask if they understand how to use them.

- Always pre-book an appointment with every client as they are checking out, even if they are unsure. They can always move it if needed. This guarantees the client will come back every 4-6 weeks.

- When products are sold, always walk the bag of products around the counter and thank the client personally.

- Have a proper POS system to run all your books, appointments, services, product sales, inventory, expected taxes, etc.

- Always keep track of records and receipts. Staying on top of things and not letting things go until tomorrow is key to front desk success.

- Send pre-book reminders 2-3 days before scheduled appointments. If the client/guest needs to move appointment times or days, you can get them back in right away with extra notice.

- Keep all client information such as emails, Facebook, Twitter in your POS system for appointments, reminders, and monthly specials, and send to all clients consistently for great results.

Each front desk professional should be trained on the services you offer. The ultimate way to train your front desk team is to have them experience the service. Create a 60-day service training commitment in your front desk training of a new team member. Make sure the service provider and the front desk team member stay focused on talking about the service. The front desk team member should take notes on what the features and benefits of the services are, as well as key hair care products that are usually recommended after the service. Finally, they should write a script on how they would offer this service to a client. Review these notes with them and role play their script. Keep these in the employee's work file.

In general, creating a script book of "Hollywood lines" for your front desk person will create consistency and ease the training process. Scripts can be created for any of the front desk guidelines listed above, such as pre-booking appointments. Again, role playing for each front desk duty involving client communication is a good teaching device for new employees.

Your front desk person should also be well-scripted and well-trained in what makes your salon "different" than the competition. Whether your salon is 8,000 square feet or 800 square feet, a salon tour is a critical place to start with a new client. Your tour can take a client on a walk through your salon, pointing out your choice of product lines, signature services, and specialists on your team. In smaller salons, this conversation may never leave the front of the salon, but still introduces the new client to who you are and what you have to offer.

Tracking and Rewarding

Implementing a goal and reward system is essential for motivating, tracking, and coaching the individuals on your front desk team. Each goal should reflect the principles and targets of growing the salon business through the front desk. The goals should be customized according to your current business trends, but be high enough to establish proper growth of your salon. Don't forget goals for these five profit principles: pre-booking, retail, referrals, gift cards, and additional services.

Implementing a goal system also requires the follow-through of a reward program. Rewards should be given monthly according to the accomplishment of the goals. Since there are five goals, there should be five levels of monthly rewards. In order to stay within budget of front desk salaries, we recommend the goals start at $15 for a level one reward and go as high as a paid day off for hitting five goals in one month.

Each individual should track their daily progress on their efforts to hit their goals. This will effectively track the sales in the success principles of additional services, gift card sales, referrals, pre-booking, and retail. Tracking provides the salon owner the opportunity to visually see their efforts, and hold the front desk individuals accountable for using their sales training and scripts in making service and retail offerings.

Salon owners or managers need to plan 30-minute meetings with each individual on the front desk team. Review tracking and make suggestions on scripts or actions to teach front desk team members how to hit goals.

If you have regular salon team meetings (and monthly meetings are recommended for a healthy, strong team culture), don't forget to recognize the front desk efforts and successes at those meetings. You can refer to the tracking sheets to quantify the efforts the front desk has made in building the salon business and service providers. Acknowledge individual goals achieved and pass out rewards at the meeting.

End Result

Marketing, advertising, and word of mouth bring valuable people into your business daily. It takes an investment of time, energy, and money to market the salon, build your brand, and secure loyal clients. Once you have a new client, your team does their very best to give great customer service and cultivate and maintain a relationship. So, why do so many salon owners hire someone without the background and skills to run and manage the front end of their business?

Most of the time, it's about the money and not thinking of the full scope of responsibilities at the front desk. Please keep in mind that you get what you pay for. Yes, this person will increase your overhead, but he or she will be worth it if you find the right person. It will also take time to train this person, but let's look at the upside. Your gatekeeper should grow into your right-hand person; in time, this is what they should be expected to do for you and your business:

- Answer phones
- Develop client relationships
- Answer routine client questions
- Order supplies
- Handle all credit and cash transactions
- Input all new clients into the system
- Manage all calls and book new appointments
- Maintain a salon "To Do List"
- Maintain office supplies and toiletries
- Handle all software updates and changes
- Initiate and assist in product sales
- Educate clients on products
- Keep clients happy while waiting
- Greet clients in a warm and friendly manner

- Thank your clients when they arrive and when they leave
- Allow you to oversee your daily salon business without major interruptions
- Deal with routine matters
- Process mail

As this person grows into his or her position, the hours that you would normally spend doing the above mentioned items should decrease dramatically. The freed-up time should be spent doing things that normally get put on the back burner, such as marketing and educating staff, and giving your clients great service while strengthening your relationship with them. More importantly, this person will enable you to spend more quality time with family and friends.

It's important to have continuous training and employee development. Either send your key people to beauty trade shows or arrange education classes in your salon through your distributor or software company. Management and/or business classes at your local high school or college can also assist in developing key people in your salon.

The key thing is, stay focused on your goals—to better serve clients, develop strong relationships with your clients, and establish better quality of life with your friends and family. The right gatekeeper will make this possible.

PART VII - SUMMARY

A 5-Star Staff

★ Your staff must be great at what they do and their attitudes and service values must reflect your own.

★ Your job is to hire, train, reward and keep a great staff with strong technical and people skills.

★ Don't forget your gatekeeper who can become your right-hand person, freeing you up to focus on your clients, the rest of your staff, and your friends and family.

★ Make your salon somewhere top-notch people want to work by providing a great facility and positive working environment.

★ Make your team want to stay by inspiring and empowering them and always showing your appreciation for their contributions.

PART VIII

KEEPING IT GOING

CHAPTER 25

Maintaining the Right Attitude

"Different is not always better, but better is always different."

—Anonymous

Y ou will hear many people talk about giving 5-star, VIP service at the salon level, and like most things, it depends on what you feel VIP service is. To some it may be coffee in a porcelain cup, to some it may be a eucalyptus foot soak prior to any spa service. VIP service is more than this, it is an attitude. And that attitude starts from the top and continues with a like-minded staff.

Whether you own a high-end salon and spa or a small hair salon, you want your Guests to feel appreciated and respected. Notice that "Guest" is capitalized. Larry Kane, owner of Jonathan Kane Salon and Spa, says that he capitalizes "Guest" in all communications with his staff and team. That sets the tone that it's all about the Guest and not about the salon team.

In his salon, they navigated through the Guest experience: what did they see when they walked in, what did they hear, smell, feel? Was it relaxing, high energy, calm, too loud, too unorganized, boring? What did the team want them to feel? Once you see what your Guests see, you can start looking at those processes and procedures that you can tweak or change that will make a difference. Keep in mind, some changes may not be eye-opening differences, but add up to a VIP experience: front line staff standing when you walk in the door, or someone to take your coat and offer fresh coffee or lemon/cucumber water. Kane's spa Guests are brought to a relaxation room to wait for their technician and to begin relaxing, rather than wait in the reception area where it is a little louder. This is where the nice coffee cup or eucalyptus foot soaks come in.

You can make the Guest Experience part of every monthly staff meeting. If your staff has the Guests' best interests in mind, they should be able to brainstorm and make additional, frequent upgrades or changes, most of them cost effective. For example, in Kane's salon, they desperately needed to paint the salon, so they held a painting party and after some potluck food and refreshments, they got it done in two days. Not one employee missed the painting party. They were all on board! One of the team members remarked, "Now it feels like our salon." The team approach added to the vibe they portray in the salon and spa as a family, a family that watches each other's back and that extends down to the clients and the services provided. That speaks to the pride of where you work and wanting what is best for the Guest.

There are some key little secrets Kane offers in the salon and spa that they feel make them different, and by different they mean better! It does not take much effort or time to implement a scalp and shoulder massage into your service cycle. Give a hot towel over the face of gentleman clients while their hair is being washed. They also condition and rinse after a short haircut so that male clients don't itch the rest of the day. For all clients, they give a hot washcloth when they sit in the styling chair just to wipe their face and hands to get off the grunge or as they call it, the wash away towel. (Wash away all the day's problems and feel cleansed and ready to start fresh and clean in the styling chair.) Now that's VIP service without even asking for it. It doesn't cost much and Guests can't wait for their hot towel when they sit in the styling chair.

When you lead, show, live, appreciate and implement a VIP attitude, it comes back. When you know what your Guests are experiencing, you know what you can improve. When you hire people who like and know how to cater to others, you know your Guests will get VIP service. By consistently giving your Guests VIP service, you'll be maintaining your 5-star difference.

CHAPTER 26

5-Star For Life

*"We are what we repeatedly do. Excellence then,
is not a single act, but a habit."*

—Aristotle

Many salon owners and stylists have the ability to cut, style, and color like nobody's business, but being successful in your career and offering 5-star service doesn't stop with the service itself—it's the entire process along the way. Many of us can be great stylists, but how many of us have the ability to offer the entire 5-star experience on a daily basis? Offering 5-star services starts one customer at a time, every time. This philosophy seems like common sense and you would think it would be easy to live up to. But it's not only you as the owner or manager that's responsible for this, it's the people you surround yourself, your salon team, that make this philosophy work or fail.

A wise leader once said that there are no individuals at work who are more important to your success and your customer's experience than your employees. You must add value by taking it personal. Your people (team) take their cue from you. You influence how they feel about the salon as a whole, about the organization, about the type of work they do, about customers, the way they dress and look, and about themselves. What you value, they will learn to value and then they will value themselves. While this may seem like a heavy burden to bear, setting the tone and modeling good service behaviors are the very essence of what leads to great service. Remember what we said earlier in the book: 5-star service starts at the top. That's you as the owner or manager. We never said this was going to be easy.

Great service leaders connect, support, enrich, and inspire their team. They also patiently listen to employees, customers, and vendors in a constant quest for service improvement. The quality of the service your salon team provides depends on the tools that you give them, from the retail products you sell, the equipment in the salon, the salon's décor and the tools you provide them for the services they provide. They rely on you as the owner or manager. The bottom line is that great service leaders achieve that status because of one overriding quality: they serve. Every time.

Keeping It Going

★ Provide 5-star service every day to every customer.

★ Make the salon focus all about the Guest.

★ Keep the customer experience in mind at all times and continually work to improve it.

★ Don't forget to also connect with, support, inspire and enrich your team.

★ Remember, being 5-star is not any single thing, it's constantly providing great service with a great team and product in a great environment!

Contributing Writers

Wallace Barlow
Master Barber / Colorist / Andis Educator / Platform Artist

Kevin Stirtz
Salon Consultant, Business Owner

Amy Carter
Empowering Your Salon Business Coach / Salon Owner

Leslie McGwire
ASID Allied Member - Leslie McGwire & Associates

Elisha Wendt
Master Colorist / Educator / Consultant - Blush Salon

Christine Dillon
Master Stylist / Educator / Consultant

Frank Zona
Owner, Zona Salons

Larry J. Kane
Owner, Jonathan Kane Salon & Spa

Arnie Cullipher
Blue Hand Home Furnishins

Jill Krahn
Senior VP of Sales, The Salon Professional Academies Franchise Group

Kristi Valenzuela
Salon Success Coach, Crystal Focus Salon Coaching

Jennifer Milspouth
Owner, Design X Manufacturing
Owner, Salon Design Specialist

Books Published by Ready, Set, Go! Publishing

For further information about the Salon and Barbershop businesses, check out the complete Ready Set Go library:

The Start-Up Guide for Opening, Remodeling & Running a Successful Beauty Salon

This book is packed with steps, tips, ideas, and strategies to make your salon a success. Whether you already own a salon or you have a glimmering thought to open one, this book will guide you through every step of opening one on time and on budget.

A Salon Owner's Guide to Wealth

Everything you need to know about selling retail and running a profitable beauty salon. Choose the right retail products to sell, marketing tips, promotions that work and point of sale tactics that will drive your business past your competitors.

The Salon Building Bible

If you plan on opening a salon or remodeling your existing one, this book includes ready-to-use floor plans, equipment costs, construction and material costs broken down to the penny, enabling you to open the salon of your dreams on time and on budget. The first book of its kind in the industry leaves you knowing exactly what it costs to open a successful beauty salon.

The Modern Salon in Pictures

Make your salon dreams reality through this salon picture book. Hundreds of award winning salon pictures from the entrance through the entire salon. Open the pages to see what salons around the globe are doing in design and furniture today and open your eyes to the possibilities for your salon.

How to Offer 5-Star Service at Your Salon and Make Big Money!

Exceptional customer service is what customers look for and expect in a salon. When it's practiced expertly and consistenty, this high level of customer service translates into customer loyalty and more revenue for your business. This book will educate you on what 5-star service in your salon should be, and is full of real examples that work.

The Start-Up Guide for Opening, Remodeling & Running a Successful Barbershop

Finally a book that brings old world barbering back with today's business strategies, barbershop design, layouts and the newest barbering equipment. Over 300 pages of expert advice to assist you with every detail of starting your new barbershop business or helping grow your existing business.

Barbershop Now!

This book leaves no stone unturned. If you are thinking about opening a barbershop business small or large this book covers every detail. Expert advice with helpful tips, recommendations and checklists to get things done and create a business model that will guarantee business success.

Cosmetology School Graduate - 1 Business Lessons

This is the first of a series of six graduate books. Learn how to make the right business decisions from paying your student loan, credit card debt, the importance of good credit and so much more. Get on the right business track to a successful career in beauty.

Cosmetology School Graduate - 2 Life Lessons

Advice from cosmetology pro's how to balance work and life, make savvy decisions, be a top performer, build great relationships, stay away from drama, and make big money in beauty.

Cosmetology School Graduate - 3 How to get a J.O.B. in a Salon

Learn from the pro's how to find job openings, interview with confidence, make a positive impression, dress for success, and land a great job and enjoy your life as a cosmetologist.

About the Authors

Jeff Grissler has been where you are and understands the inner workings of the salon industry and what leads to success as a salon owner. As a business owner, he understands the business landscape and what owners can expect and guides them to success. Jeff is a partner of and the National Sales Manager for Quest Resources—one of the salon industry's leading financing companies for furniture and equipment. His career in finance began on Wall Street and he has been involved in the multimillion dollar beauty industry for over 20 years. Jeff has financed over 15,000 salons to help them open their doors or complete their remodeling project through creative financing strategies.

Published in many beauty trade magazines, Jeff is setting a new business standard in the beauty industry as we see it today. Jeff has a beauty portfolio of over 600 million dollars in salon financing and a network of over 150 manufacturers, distributors, and vendors. A gifted businessman and consultant, Jeff prides himself on his networking ability to bring people together to share new ideas and explore partnerships and marketing techniques. Through his skilled negotiations, he has convinced the banking industry to lift restrictions from the beauty industry. He has also negotiated contracts and leases with salon owners, spa owners, distributors, manufacturers, and banking management.

Jeff was born in New York City before moving to the Jersey Shore. He was a New York City fireman for 15+ years and served during 911. Jeff now resides in Wilmington, NC with his wife, Coleen, and their three children—Kaytlyn, JT, and Julianna Rose.

Jeff offers consulting services to current salon owners and to those who have salon ownership in their near-term or future career plans. To reach Jeff, you can contact him directly at jgrissler@questrs.com.

Eric Ryant is a beauty industry entrepreneur with over 30 years of experience in space-planning and design for salons. No stranger to the salon industry, Eric spent many years developing new designs and space plans, getting involved in every facet of the industry. Since the 1980s, Eric has imported salon furniture from many countries, such as Italy, Germany, Holland, and China, bringing in the latest trends and styles for the U.S. market.

Prior to writing this book, Eric owned several successful businesses, all involved in the salon industry, from a small chain of beauty stores to a cabinet manufacturing facility. He has also collaborated with companies such as Sally Beauty Supply, L'Oreal, and The Nailco Group.

Eric's vision is to help clients create their dream salon with a cost-effective business model and ensure that they stay within budget for the long haul. As part of his successful career, he now teaches and consults with other organizations on how to achieve the same success. Eric can be reached at ericryant@gmail.com.

Made in the USA
Charleston, SC
23 December 2013